Praise for *Newbies in the Cafe*

Congrats on a fantastic book!!
From the layout, the real stories with great insights, the quality of writing and finally the last chapter that brings it all together, it is perfect.
This book will certainly help many people understand what the industry is all about and provide some great insights and foresights.
I believe it should be a must for all to read BEFOFE they enter the world of cafe ownership so that they move into it with their eyes wide open.

Phillip Di Bella
Chairman, Di Bella Group of Companies

The journey into cafe ownership can be a dream come true or your worst nightmare. While no one can predict how their own journey will turn out, they can learn from the hindsight of others who've trodden the track.

Reading this book is like having brutally honest conversations with 11 cafe owners. You'll learn the secrets to their success, the reasons for their fast track to failure, the pitfalls they could have avoided, the surprises they encountered along the way, whether buying an existing cafe or opening one from scratch was the best option for them – and so much more, right down to whether they were cut out to be a cafe owner or not.

Each story is so engaging; you feel you're on the journey already – learning what working in a cafe is really like, empowered to make informed decisions about your own cafe.

In the last chapter, the author (one of the cafe owners featured) draws together what she and the 10 others have learnt – in 20 pages of the best advice you're ever likely to get about running a cafe.

Christine Cottrell
Author of the BARISTA BIBLE and
TRENDING CAFES Brisbane & Beyond

A 'textbook style' masterpiece!!

In my 15-year cafe journey I have never found such complete and concise information all in one place.

Brutally honest and refreshingly real, the stories are captivating, sometimes tragic, yet filled with lessons for the next wave of cafe newbies.

Finally, a 'warts and all' work to counter the fable that's sold as … The Cafe Dream.

If you're contemplating a cafe then read it! … (SEVERAL TIMES!!)

Simon O'Brien
Cafe Coach, Kickstart Coffee Shop

One of the greatest factors that affects success in this industry is support.

This book not only provides this from examples of people in the industry today, but is extremely easy to digest, gives professional insight and guidance – for the newcomer right through to the elite.

Joshua Clifton
Author of THE HOSPITALITY SURVIVAL GUIDE

NEWBIES
IN THE CAFE

Lessons from behind the counter

Dr Judy Gregory

First published in Australia in 2020 by Judy Gregory

Website: www.newbiesinthecafe.com.au

Email for correspondence: judy@judygregorywriter.com.au

© Judy Gregory 2020

All rights reserved.

Apart from any fair dealing for the purpose of study, research, criticism or review as permitted under the Copyright Act, no part may be reproduced by any process without prior written permission.

All enquiries should be directed to the author.

ISBN 9780648703808 (paperback)

 A catalogue record for this book is available from the National Library of Australia

Disclaimer

The author has made every effort to ensure the information in this book was correct at the time of publication.

Typesetting and cover design by Brisbane Self Publishing Service
Edited by PS Editing

Cover illustration

A line drawing of a La Marzocco Linea PB, pouring a 22 g, 30 second dose of Elixir's espresso blend at The Letter Lounge Cafe & Gifts in 2017. Imagine our endlessly cheerful and competent barista, Val, behind the machine, using the left wand (not her favourite) to texture the milk for a cappuccino and flat white. Illustration by Anne-Maree Jaggs.

For Anne-Maree – who is always a willing participant in my dreams and big ideas.

Contents

Introduction   1
1   The lure of the cafe   5
2   It helps if you like the work   17
3   Let the buyer beware!   34
4   Dream big, work hard, love the work   44
5   A four-year foray into the coffee shop world   54
6   The accidental cafe   71
7   It's not work when you love the industry   81
8   From nothing to success and back again   92
9   Start small + grow slow = a recipe for success   103
10   But where are the customers?   112
11   From the university to the cafe and back again   123
12   For the love of people   145
13   Lessons from the newbies   157
Appendix 1: Business plan headings   179
Appendix 2: Financial targets and ratios   182
Appendix 3: Promotion plan headings and ideas   184
Appendix 4: Staff manual headings   186
Acknowledgements   189
About Judy Gregory   191

Introduction

The idea for this book started to form in mid-2017, when I was out of my depth and unsure where to turn. I wondered then whether reading other people's stories might help me understand my own.

In mid-2017, my partner Anne-Maree and I had been living our dream business for about 15 months. I felt stuck in a situation that I hadn't anticipated, with no idea how to escape. Anne-Maree was already tired of hearing me say: 'I'm so sorry I got us into this. I had no idea it would be like this'.

We were the 'proud' owners of Northside Meetings with The Letter Lounge Cafe & Gifts. We had a cute word-themed cafe that sold home-style food. We had a little shop that sold literary and word-themed gifts. And we had a meetings venue with rooms for hire – three smallish rooms and one large training room.

We could see that our business was growing. By August 2017 – the month I turned 50 – our takings reached almost 85 per cent of our break-even target. But 85 per cent still left us 15 per cent short, and that money had to come from somewhere.

I propped the shop up with my consulting. Somehow, I managed to write and edit documents for clients while working in the cafe, organising events, doing the roster, and paying the bills. I'd spend my time hidden away in the shop's little office, working on documents for clients – until the cafe bell rang and I'd run to the front to serve customers, plate a meal, or clear tables.

By mid-2017, I'd stopped thinking ahead to our original goal – which was to enjoy building the business for about 10 years and then sell it. I simply focused on how to survive each day. The only thing that kept me going was knowing that the shop would close for three weeks at Christmas, and that we'd pre-paid for a two-week holiday at the beach. I got myself to sleep each night by imagining I was walking on the beach.

I was too stressed to make sensible decisions. But I figured that if our monthly losses were less than the cost of rent then it made sense to keep the shop open. Sometimes I imagined that I might run away. Often, I wondered what the next crisis would bring. But mostly I just worked without thinking.

Understanding the cafe dream

Throughout 2017, I used networking to build our business, and I tried to attend at least one networking function a week. If I found a networking opportunity that might introduce me to potential clients for our meetings venue, I'd be there.

It was at networking events that I started to understand the cafe dream. It seemed that every time I entered a room of strangers, I'd find people with a cafe story to tell. Many were cafe dreamers who seemed envious of our journey – they seemed to think that a cafe would bring them the lifestyle they craved. Others had tried cafe ownership for a while, then moved on. Occasionally, I met someone who had experienced long-term cafe success. What I noticed was that everyone with cafe experience had something to share about what they'd learned.

After we closed The Letter Lounge in mid-2018, I started to pay more attention to the cafe stories I found on social media. I continued to participate in cafe owners' groups and barista groups, and I noticed many cafe newbies asking for advice. That's when I decided to put together a collection of stories about cafe newbies. I wanted to share real stories, real dreams, and real experiences.

Introduction

I put out a call on social media seeking people who had started or bought a cafe following a career doing something else. I invited them to tell their stories and share things they know now that they wish they'd known before opening. More than 30 people responded to my call, and I've collected 10 of their stories for this book.

This isn't a book about why you should or shouldn't open a cafe. It's a book of shared experiences, and it ends with our combined lessons. The idea behind the book is that sharing other people's stories is a powerful way of understanding your own.

I hope this book will give you some insight into the complexity and diversity of the cafe business. I hope it will help you to understand your own situation and make your own decisions. I hope it will help you reflect on how you got where you are and how you can create the path ahead.

I wish I'd had this book before I opened my cafe and meetings venue. There's no chance this book would have stopped me from starting my dream business, but it might have opened my eyes a little. It might have helped me take things more slowly or find a way to test the experience before committing everything.

I remain convinced that you can't know in advance whether your business will succeed. And you can't know in advance what the experience will be like. It's only hindsight that helps you understand a little about why things turned out the way they did. I hope that you can use the hindsight collected in this book to help with your own business decisions.

If you're a cafe dreamer, then I wish you well. If this book leaves you confident that a cafe is the right business for you, then that's fabulous. If you make a good long black, I'll be there in a flash.

What you'll find in this book

Newbies in the Cafe is a book of stories about cafe dreamers who have taken the plunge into cafe ownership following a successful career in another discipline. In the following chapters, you'll meet:

- Me and my partner Anne-Maree Jaggs – who established The Letter Lounge Cafe & Gifts in Brisbane in 2016
- Cheryl Cornish – a former vocational trainer who bought Get Tossed, a salad bar–cafe in Albury, in late 2017
- Alex Milosovic – a former steel fabricator who opened Extraction, Logan City's first artisan coffee roastery and cafe, in 2016
- Jen Robertson and Terri Kerr – who established the cafe Giggles in Brisbane's western suburbs in the late 1990s, following careers in retail and administration
- Anne Roussac-Hoyne – an editor, gallery owner, and former French teacher who opened Cow Cow in Foster near Wilsons Promontory in late 2018
- Anthea Williams – a former university manager who opened a cafe in the Adelaide suburb of Forestville in 2012 and now operates Keswick Cafe within Adelaide's Keswick Barracks
- A person I'm calling Aimee – a former hydrogeologist who established a cafe and roastery in regional Australia in 2002
- Reg James – who left a career in retail to set up Bay21 in the Melbourne suburb of Forest Hill in 2018
- Neill Hooper – a former advertising executive who established Haven Espresso in the Brisbane suburb of Stafford Heights in 2014
- Kylie Turville – who in 2012 opened a gift shop–cafe in Linton in rural Victoria following a long career as a lecturer in information technology
- Narelle Adams – who worked in childcare and studied business before opening Country Heart in the Yarra Valley, with a cafe in Mooroolbark, a moveable coffee-caravan, and a farm-wedding venue.

The closing chapter combines our experiences into a baker's dozen of lessons for cafe newbies. If you're gripped by the cafe dream and you're seriously considering that you might take the plunge into cafe ownership, this is the chapter for you.

Chapter 1

The lure of the cafe

The cafe dream: And why it grips so many adults

The cafe scene: The place of independent cafes

Cafe success: Common causes of success and failure

NEWBIES IN THE CAFE

The morning rush

It's 7:30 am, right in the middle of your morning rush. The queue is out the door, and your front-of-house staff take orders as quickly as possible. You're working the machine. Grind, tamp, attach, extract, froth, pour, present. You've got your rhythm and you're pumping out coffees at a rate that's keeping pace with the orders. A few regulars stop for a chat and a laugh. This is your happy place. Your cafe is the centre of the world, with you at the helm. You're living your dream.

The morning nightmare

It's 10:00 am and your cafe is empty – other than the guy hunched over his laptop in the far corner who has been sitting on a flat white for almost two hours. You can just tell he's giving the wi-fi a beating. You haven't touched the grinder for 30 minutes and there's no sign of any change afoot. The cabinet is stocked with fresh food that will see the bin if it's not sold by closing time. There was no morning rush today and you realise that your morning rush is becoming increasingly patchy. If the day continues like it started, you'll be lucky to take $200 – not even enough to cover the wages. All the other daily costs – the rent, electricity, coffee beans, and food – will be coming from your pocket. What happened to the dream? This cafe is starting to feel like an expensive hobby.

The cafe dream

The dream of cafe ownership is popular and compelling:

It'll be like hosting a permanent coffee catch-up with friends. An environment that encourages people to congregate and linger. Fresh coffee, made just right. Perfect food, crafted with care. Just the right balance of tradition and innovation. Time to talk with customers, get to know the regulars, and craft the perfect plate. Friendly staff who enjoy their work. The best elements of every cafe you've ever visited, combined in one place. And it will be all yours.

Chapter 1: The lure of the cafe

The cafe dream comes in several varieties:
- Maybe it's a themed cafe – like a cat cafe, a Star Wars cafe, a literary cafe, a Harry Potter cafe or one of the world's increasing number of board game cafes
- Maybe it's a cafe integrated into another business – like a book shop, a gift shop, a day spa, or a co-working space
- Maybe it's a niche cafe – a place that sells artisanal coffee or specialty tea, or a vegan cafe, or its polar opposite the paleo cafe
- Maybe it's a simple independent cafe that meets the needs and tastes of its local community.

The cafe dream seems to capture most adults at some time or another. It's a dream that doesn't discriminate: it targets people with and without industry experience, people with and without money, people from every profession, people at any age. The cafe dream captured me: an academic and writer with an established consultancy business. It captures lawyers, engineers, social workers, business analysts, sports players, government bureaucrats, and others. Many leave well-paying jobs to chase their dream.

Most people captured by the cafe dream recognise that hospitality is hard work. But they see it as honest work – real work, with a stable income. Profit margins are guaranteed if you understand basic maths. After all, it's not rocket science. There's a cafe on every corner, and they're all busy. How hard can it be?

Only a small percentage of the people captured by the dream actually act on it. Of those, some establish successful, profitable businesses they love. Others find themselves drowning in chaos and robbed of their savings, health, and relationships.

Cafe success or failure seems near-impossible to predict. While pre-planning, industry experience, and access to capital are all helpful, there's no good evidence they're determinants of success. If there's a 'magic ingredient', it remains elusive.

My partner and I closed our cafe after 26 months of difficult operation. The pre-cafe dream lasted longer than the cafe reality. In the end, it simply became too much for us, and we didn't want to continue. But our cafe experience got me thinking: are there lessons for others to learn from the experiences of newbies who decide to act on their cafe dreams? In the months since our cafe closed, I've spoken to many cafe newbies. We share our stories here – to inspire and motivate other newbies and to help you learn from our experiences.

The place of the cafe

In times gone by, people gathered in places like village squares, markets, and churches. Today, those people are more likely to meet in a cafe. Cafes (plus perhaps shopping centres) are the places where we meet, chat, and share hospitality.

This isn't new: cafes have always been meeting places. The first cafes were meeting places for the few – for society's elite or intelligentsia. Today's cafes are meeting places for everyone.

More than 500 years ago, people gathered in the coffee houses of Mecca to discuss politics. In the 1680s, Edward Lloyd founded Lloyds of London while working from one of his own cafes. Throughout history, philosophers, scientists, artists, intellectuals, and political radicals have used cafes as places for meetings and debate. In seventeenth century England, cafes became known as 'penny universities': for the price of a cup of coffee, you could listen to cutting-edge debates and new ideas.[1]

Today, cafes are linked to urbanisation and modern life.[2] They're an integral part of the city and the suburb, places that offer both social interaction and social solitude. People meet in cafes – for work meetings, job interviews, special-interest groups, social occasions, and family time. People also spend time alone in cafes – working, reading, writing, or simply watching the world go by.

The opportunity to 'be alone in public' is part of cafes' attraction.[3] They've been described as 'third spaces' – places of rest and recuperation where people can escape from daily life in a place that is not home (the first space) and not work (the second space).[4]

What's so great about the cafe?

Cafes offer advantages not available in other places. To start with, they're widely accessible and welcoming. They invite leisurely visits and a near-suspension of the passage of time. Instead of feeling pressured to leave quickly, cafe customers usually feel welcome to linger long after their cup is empty. The comfortable environment invites them to stay.

Cafes are highly affordable. They offer what industry reports describe as an 'affordable indulgence'[5] – they sell drinks and food that most people consider to be special and something they're unlikely to have at home, but what they sell is within the budget of most.

Cafes are widely seen as 'safe' spaces, particularly for single women. They're places where people tend to feel comfortable, whether alone or with others. Most cafes welcome a diverse group of customers and, most importantly, welcome young children. Cafes have taken over some of the roles traditionally held by pubs, providing meeting spaces that aren't based around alcohol.[6]

Many cafes deliberately invite people to use them as a space for work. The lure of the cafe-as-office – described by some as the 'coffice' – is fuelled by mobile technology that enables people to work almost anywhere.[7] Home-based freelancers and people working for distributed companies (where employees work from their homes or vehicles) often set themselves up for extended work time in cafes that offer free wi-fi and easy access to power. They might stay for several hours, perhaps alternating between meetings and quiet working time. But, as Ward points out, the 'coffice' creates a dilemma for the cafe: it's only successful for cafes if workers continue to buy food and drink. A customer who buys one coffee in a six-hour visit will not help pay the bills.[8]

Cafes in Australia

Cafes come in many different styles and types – from large franchises, chains, and cafes attached to fast-food outlets, through to small independents. While chains and franchises capture a large chunk of the market in the UK and USA, in Australia it's small, independent cafes that are most common. Australia's coffee scene is recognised as amongst the world's best, with Australian-style cafes appearing in many countries.[9]

The classic Australian cafe is a one-shop operation employing fewer than 20 staff. It's likely to emphasise quality over quantity, with an increasing focus on artisanal coffee roasts and various brewing methods. Industry experts suggest that customers in Australia choose independent cafes because they value variety, quality, tailored coffee, and broad product offerings.[10]

According to the IBIS*World* Industry Report, Australia had 20,781 cafes in early 2019, with the industry experiencing around 2.5 per cent growth over the previous five years.[11] IBIS*World* predicts that growth will continue, though more slowly. It describes the cafe industry as risky, with low barriers to entry and high competition.

The largest player in Australia's cafe industry controls less than three per cent of the national market (based on early 2019 figures). It's Retail Food Group, which operates Gloria Jean's Coffees, Michel's Patisserie, Cafe2U, and Di Bella Coffee. Its industry share dropped between 2018 and 2019.[12] Its growth has also slowed, with most of its expansion coming from acquisitions rather than new cafe openings. In 2019 it closed several franchise stores.[13]

The world's largest cafe chain, Starbucks, first arrived in Australia in the early 2000s. While Starbucks initially grew quickly in Australia, it was unable to establish significant market share and closed several stores in 2008. In 2014, the Australian rights to Starbucks were bought by Withers Group (which also owns 7-Eleven in Australia) and a second round of expansion started. In 2018, Starbucks held less than 1 per cent of the Australian cafe market.[14]

The Starbucks' experience demonstrates the difficulties faced by cafe chains in Australia. IBIS*World* suggests that successful cafes demonstrate an understanding of their local coffee culture and provide a coffee experience that meets consumer preferences.[15] And localisation may be the key: coffee lovers commonly discuss, for example, the differences between the coffee available in Melbourne, Sydney, and Brisbane. With consumers increasingly seeking locally roasted beans, small-batch coffee, rare blends, fair trade, and organics, this trend is likely to continue.

Cafe success and failure

Everyone agrees the cafe industry is tough. The work is hard. The hours are long. The expenses are relentless. The profit margins are small. Yet new cafes open every week, fuelled by the cafe dream and their owners' enthusiasm.

The statistics reporting cafe failure vary. It is widely accepted that most new cafes fail within their first three years. A University of Technology Sydney (UTS) report suggests that one in three cafes fail in their first year, and three in four fail within five years.[16] An Australian cafe coach, Rita Zhang, suggests that 70 per cent of cafes fail within the first year, most cafes change hands every two to three years, and more than 50 per cent of the businesses for sale are food related.[17]

When I combined the industry growth statistics from IBIS*World* with the estimates of cafe failure from UTS, I concluded that Australian consumers must welcome around 500 successful new cafes each year. To achieve this, close to 2,000 cafes must open each year. Of these, around 166 will close in the first year and 1,500 will close within five years.

So why do some cafes succeed in the face of widespread failure?

The honest answer is that no one knows. As McBride writes, there's no magic formula, and no clear reason why some cafes will succeed while others fail.[18]

Various industry reports and business guides suggest that three issues may be key factors in cafe failure:

1. *Seeing cafes as a lifestyle business*: Many cafe dreamers focus on the lifestyle they seek, and forget that cafes are hard work with continual expenses and great potential for things to go wrong.[19] People who enter the industry with no hospitality experience are at particular risk. This problem was captured by chef Anthony Bourdain in his book *Kitchen Confidential* when he commented that the most 'dangerous species of owner … is the one who gets into the industry for love'.[20]

2. *Financial mismanagement or inexperience*: Many new cafe owners struggle with the financial side of their business. Some estimates suggest that 32 per cent of cafe failures can be linked to poor financial management.[21] Like all businesses, cafes involve a combination of fixed costs (like rent and insurance), variable costs (like coffee beans, food, and wages), and highly variable income. Coordinating the variable income with the variable costs is an ongoing challenge. Successful cafe owners are likely to understand, at a minimum, their break-even points and percentages (e.g., How much does the cafe need to take each day to cover basic costs? How many kilograms of coffee each week is the minimum for viability? What is the relationship between coffee sales and food sales?). Idov suggests it makes sense to allocate 25 per cent for rent, 25 per cent for payroll, 35 per cent for product, and 15 per cent for you.[22] In my cafe planning, I figured that, to break even, my coffee target was 19 kilograms per week, my coffee sales target was 40 per cent of turnover, and my food ingredient cost target was 12 per cent of sale price. Knowing these figures didn't make me successful, but they helped me understand the source of my pain.

3. *Lack of planning*: When people are caught up in a dream, it's difficult to take the time to plan. And while planning doesn't guarantee success, it can certainly set you off in the right direction. According to UTS, fewer than 5 per cent of cafe owners develop a detailed business plan before opening.[23] Without a plan, cafe owners

are unlikely to give sufficient thought to the business basics – such as risk assessment, staffing needs, medium- and long-term goals, profitability, and sales targets.

Annette Freeman's Tea in the Library

In the late 1990s, Sydney-based trademarks lawyer Annette Freeman opened Tea in the Library, a hybrid book shop–cafe. Her book about the experience was published in 2007.[24]

Freeman's book describes her long-term dream of owning a cosy bookshop that served great coffee and specialty tea, and hosted literary events, discussion groups, and book clubs. She spent extensive time planning and researching her dream before opening her shop, a basement in York Street Sydney opposite the Queen Victoria Building.

As a lawyer, Freeman believed in the value of research and planning. She learned about the industry. She wrote a careful business plan. She employed consultants to guide her along the way. And she heard the dire warnings about new businesses failure. According to Freeman, those warnings were about as successful as the health warnings on cigarette packets. She was addicted to the idea of her book shop–cafe. She understood that it would be hard work, but she was convinced that her business would be the one to succeed.

Freeman's book describes her experiences in the 18 months that Tea in the Library remained open. Freeman continued to work in her day job as a lawyer, funding the shop's ongoing losses. The shop was fully staffed, but it was Freeman who handled the ongoing problems with profitability, staffing, stock rotation, and poor sales. Freeman employed a network of advisors and consultants, including a business coach, public relations consultant, and accountant.

Freeman closed Tea in the Library when she finally accepted that she could no longer afford to pour money into the shop and when she heard complaints from her legal colleagues about her divided attention. In her book she explains that it was a difficult decision:

although the shop was never financially viable, she was immensely proud of what she created.

Towards the end of her book, Freeman questions whether her decision to keep the security of her day job led to the demise of the book shop–cafe. She needed a regular income to meet repayments on the loan she'd taken out to set up the shop. But if she'd been working in the shop full-time, would it have been successful? It's a question she'll never be able to answer.

Freeman identifies a dilemma faced by many people who dream of starting a business. Passion is a vital ingredient to business success. Without passion, the business will never become a reality. But the very passion that underpins success can also set the owner up to fail. Passion may obscure the need for a hard-headed attitude to profitability, and obscure clear thinking about the challenges ahead.

Michael Idov's bitter experience

In 2005, Michael Idov, a staff writer with *New York Magazine*, wrote a short article for *Slate* about his disastrous experience opening a small cafe in New York.[25]

He reflected on the cafe dream, suggesting that it's based on a desire to host endless dinner parties for friends rather than any real understanding of the business reality. Based on his experience, Idov suggests that cafe failure isn't linked to the owners' competence. Instead, he describes failure as a 'sad given', with owners highly likely to lose a lot of money. Idov argues that the logistics of a small cafe mean the business can only stay open if the owners work long hours for very little income.

Idov received more than 500 emails after his article in *Slate*, most of them full of cafe woes.[26] Inspired by the emails, he wrote a novel based on his experience – *Ground Up: A Novel*.[27] In the novel, his characters Mark and Nina are determined to open the perfect cafe and end up on a downward spiral that strips them of their friends, money, home, and relationship.

Chapter 1: The lure of the cafe

References

1. Felton, Emma. 2019. *Filtered. Coffee, the Cafe and the 21st Century City*. Abingdon UK: Routledge. Ward, Chris. 2013. *Out of Office: Work Where You Like and Achieve More*. London: Blue Dot World.
2. Felton. op. cit. Tjora, Aksel & Scrambler, Graham. (Eds.). 2013. *Cafe Society*. New York: Palgrave Macmillan.
3. Walters, Peter & Broom, Alex. 2013. The city, the cafe, and the public realm in Australia. In Tjora, Aksel & Scrambler, Graham (Eds.). *Cafe Society* (pp. 185–205). New York: Palgrave Macmillan.
4. Oldenburg, Ray. 2013. The cafe as a third place. In Tjora, Aksel & Scrambler, Graham (Eds.). *Cafe Society* (pp. 7–21). New York: Palgrave Macmillan.
5. Vuong, Bao. 2019, May. *IBISWorld Industry Report H4511b: Cafes and Coffee Shops in Australia*.
6. Ferriera, Jennifer. 2017. Cafe nation? Exploring the growth of the UK cafe industry. *Area, 49*(1), 69–76. doi: 10.1111/area.12285
7. Ward. op. cit.
8. ibid.
9. Vuong. op cit.
10. ibid.
11. ibid.
12. The January 2018 IBIS*World* Industry Report reported the Retail Food Group held 4.8% of the market. In the May 2019 report, Retail Food Group's share had dropped below 3%.
13. Vuong. op. cit.
14. Vuong. 2018, January. *IBISWorld Industry Report H4511b: Cafes and Coffee Shops in Australia*.
15. Vuang. 2019. op.cit.
16. *Start Me Up Guide*. 2005. Sydney: University of Technology Sydney. Available: https://www.uts.edu.au/sites/default/files/Start_me_up.pdf. Accessed 11 November 2018.

17. Zhang, Rita. No date. *11 Biggest Mistakes Most People Make When Buying a Cafe or Coffee Shop.* Unpublished report. Available: https://www.cafe-coach.com.au. Accessed 7 March 2019.
18. McBride, Sean. 2017, October 5. *Uniqueness in Your Restaurant or Cafe.* Copper Pantry Consulting [Blog post]. Available: https://www.copperpantry.com.au/blog/uniqueness-restaurant-cafe-major-factor-contributes-failure-hospitality-businesses/. Accessed: 11 November 2018.
19. Bowen, Claire. 2018. *13 Reasons Coffee Shops Fail.* Presentation to Caffé Culture 2019. London Business Design Centre. Transcript available:https://www.cafesuccesshub.com/13-reason-coffee-shops-fail-caffe-culture-2018/. Accessed 28 November 2018.
20. Bourdain, Anthony. 2013. *Kitchen Confidential.* London: Bloomsbury.
21. *Start Me Up Guide.* op. cit.
22. Idov, Michael. 2005, December 29. Bitter Brew. *Slate.* Available: https://slate.com/human-interest/2005/12/my-coffeehouse-nightmare.html. Accessed 6 November 2018.
23. *Start Me Up Guide.* op. cit.
24. Freeman, Annette. 2007. *Tea in the Library.* Hartwell, Australia: Sid Harta Publishers.
25. Idov. op. cit.
26. La Force, Thessaly. 2009, August 11. The Exchange: Michael Idov. *The New Yorker.* Available: https://www.newyorker.com/books/page-turner/the-exchange-michael-idov. Accessed 6 November 2018.
27. Idov, Michael. 2009. *Ground Up: A Novel.* New York: Farrar, Straus and Giroux.

Chapter 2

It helps if you like the work

Newbie: Me (Judy Gregory) and Anne-Maree Jaggs

Cafe: Northside Meetings with The Letter Lounge Cafe & Gifts, Red Hill Qld (2016 – 2018)

Previous occupation: Writer/editor/researcher (me) and university administrator (Anne-Maree)

NEWBIES IN THE CAFE

On 1 March 2016, my partner Anne-Maree and I opened our dream business: Northside Meetings with The Letter Lounge Cafe & Gifts.

It was a quirky, word-themed cafe, with home-style cooking, handmade cakes, great coffee, and leaf tea. The food and drinks were themed around words and books: think of 'Scone with the Wind' and 'To Kill a Muffinbird', and you're on the right track.

The cafe was attached to a small gift shop, which sold word-themed gifts and cards. If a gift item included words or a literary message, we were keen to stock it.

Sitting behind the cafe was the 'real' business – a venue where people could run meetings, events, and training. We had three private meeting rooms and one large training room for hire, all equipped with AV equipment and meeting-room needs, and which were serviced by the cafe.

Anne-Maree and I invested many years preparing for the business. We planned everything, right down to the ways we would take bookings, greet customers, and arrange cakes on the plate.

But nothing prepared us for the difficulties involved in starting the business from scratch. And nothing prepared us for the sad reality that we didn't much like the work.

In May 2018 we closed the business. After 26 months of struggle and stress, and after accumulating more than $500,000 of debt, we decided to call it quits.

The dream's origin

I'm a writer and editor who specialises in using simple language to explain complex ideas. For many years, I worked at Queensland University of Technology as a lecturer in communication. In 2005, I left the university and set myself up as an independent writer, editor, and trainer.

My partner, Anne-Maree, is a trained artist who was working in university administration and hoping for a change that would bring more creativity into her work.

I made a good income as a consultant, working mostly in the government, community, and university sectors. A big part of my work was training in workplace writing and, from 2010, I started to think about ways to offer training to individuals by advertising public courses.

It was through my writing training that I noticed Brisbane was lacking an affordable, practical, independent training space. I tried hotels, but found them boring and expensive. I tried community centres, but found them lacking the professional edge I wanted. I tried libraries, but found their meeting-room systems difficult and their venues lacking in flexibility. I tried schools, and they worked well for weekend training if I was happy to organise my own catering supplies. What I wanted was a reasonably priced, independent space that offered good equipment and great catering.

And so, our dream was born. We began to spend our spare time discussing our vision for a hybrid meeting venue and cafe. In September 2012, while on holiday at Caloundra, I bought a beautiful notebook and began some serious research and brainstorming. In March 2013, I had my first tentative conversations with a coffee company, an IT consultant, a business coach, and my accountant.

Anne-Maree and I planned and schemed, and planned and schemed some more. We were obsessed, and probably bored everyone with our ideas, questions, and vision. We were determined to make the dream a reality.

Slow, careful planning

As a researcher and writer, I knew that I needed to do my planning. I started by researching the industry, talking to everyone I could find, and developing a detailed business plan. My research suggested there was a real appetite in Brisbane for the business I had in mind.

I fitted the planning around my consulting work and some serious financial preparation. We saved hard and paid off our house. While we didn't have any cash savings, we had a reasonable income and a solid asset in our house. Our idea was to borrow money to get started, operate the business for around 10 years, and then sell. We fully expected that selling the business would pay off the original loan and fund our retirement.

My dream was to continue with my writing consultancy while working in the business as its overall supervisor. I didn't imagine myself working long-term in the cafe or handling venue enquiries. But I recognised my need to understand every aspect of the work, and I was ready to be fully involved for the first few months.

We decided that Anne-Maree would continue working part-time at the university to provide us with a secure income. We imagined that she would eventually manage the venue side of the business and return to her long-forgotten artwork.

We both have extensive experience in managing events and meetings, so we were confident that the venue side of the business would cause us little trouble. Our hospitality experience was limited; we'd both done hospitality work as teenagers, but nothing since. We addressed that problem with our research and our plans to employ experienced staff. For some reason, we expected that this business would leave us with more time to do the things we enjoyed and more time to spend with our family.

During the planning phase, I read widely about the cafe industry and the venue industry. I read about business strategy, and attended every business advice and business networking meeting I could find. I was on a mission to both learn about business and to expand my networks (because those networks would become my promotional leverage once the business opened).

I clearly remember sitting at a business networking breakfast, listening to Phillip Di Bella, a highly successful cafe entrepreneur, talking about risk. His advice was to decide whether you were ready to 'make friends' with the financial risks you were taking. He advised that anyone unable to accept the worst possible financial outcome should not go into business. Anne-Maree and I understood that we were risking our main asset – our house. We thought that we had 'made friends' with the risk. What we didn't realise at the time was that a risk on paper is quite different from the real experience. We also didn't realise that there's only a tiny space between business success and business failure.

By late 2014, I had written a detailed business plan (70+ pages), complete with a marketing plan and financial forecasts. I'd spent time with my accountant, who could see no reason why the financial forecasts were seriously flawed. I shared the business plan with several trusted colleagues and with people who worked in the cafe industry. I inspected many potential sites and was struggling to find a suitable location.

Making the dream a reality

At the end of 2014, I realised the dream would never become a reality if I didn't cut back on my other work. I decided to continue with consulting, but left the one-day-a-week research-advice position I had at a local university. Then things started to happen more quickly. By January 2015, we had a mortgage broker helping us to secure a loan, a leasing broker helping us to find premises, and a cafe consultant helping us to understand the industry.

My first learning in 2015 was that consultants don't necessarily do anything you can't do yourself, and they often come with a high price tag. Employing a leasing broker was a mistake. By the time I contracted them, I already had good links with several property agents. I was beginning to see that my original vision, for around 600 m^2 of space, was too ambitious and too expensive.

One day in early 2015, I drove past a little shop in Brisbane's Red Hill with a 'for lease' sign on the roof. I contacted the leasing agent and found myself inside a gorgeous character building that could easily house the business we had in mind. At 250 m^2, it was smaller than our dream building, but it had exactly the right character and spaces that could be made to work. We parted with the leasing broker and negotiated independently with the owner.

A dream project

From Easter 2015 until February 2016, we were caught in the excitement of getting the project off the ground.

To start with, we secured our bank loan and negotiated a hold on the building. The building owner agreed to give us nine months to organise development approval for a change of use and finalise our renovation plans. I worked closely with a town planner, architect, and builder to make this happen. Development approval came through in November 2015 and we took over the lease in January 2016.

I also spent 2015 in even more detailed planning and preparation. I completed a food safety course and a barista course, and wrote our procedures manuals, staff handbooks, promotional materials, and anything else I thought we would need. In late 2015 we developed our logo and branding, and began to develop our promotional materials.

Renovations began when we took over the lease in January 2016, and the race was on to open as quickly as possible. We installed a commercial kitchen, knocked out walls to open up the cafe space, removed nine structural poles from the training room downstairs, and ensured that every aspect of the building complied with regulations. Our approvals came through easily, and the cafe was opened as planned on 1 March 2016. The finished meeting rooms followed a few weeks later.

Managing the project was perhaps the most enjoyable, stimulating, rewarding thing I have ever worked on. Everything went according to plan and cost roughly what I expected. We worked with wonderful contractors who turned our dreams into a reality. And while we didn't have money to throw around, we definitely had enough to do the renovations required. We were confident that our investment in the building would pay off, and we believed we had enough cash left in the loan to see us through the difficult first months. We expected to break even in four to six months, and reach a turnover approaching $1 million within about two years.

Opening the business

Nothing prepared us for the shock we encountered when we opened. Looking back, I can see that we were caught up in the dream and unprepared for several issues that left us floundering. I've identified seven problems that left us in a constant state of crisis and confusion.

1. Lack of confidence

I'm one of those people who works hard and is reasonably satisfied with the outcomes I produce, but always believes that someone else is doing a better job than me. I've always felt that others know things I don't know and understand things I don't understand. I also know that I come across as confident, so most people have no idea at the terror sitting beneath my calm exterior. As a consultant and university educator, I could always put in the hours needed to feel reasonably confident that I was doing a good job. And I can always be relied on to take the effort that's needed and deliver on time.

But I quickly discovered that the cafe environment is not the right workplace for someone with my temperament. Like most new cafe owners, I needed to work in every aspect of the business – I served customers, prepared food, washed dishes, and cleared tables. I also worked in every aspect of the venue – I set up meeting rooms, provided catering, organised AV equipment, and answered every whim of the people using the space.

I found myself, from day one, troubled that my customer service was too slow, my coffee wasn't perfect, my cream wasn't whipped just right, and my scones were just a little flat. I worried that we were too noisy in the kitchen (disturbing the guests). I worried that we were too slow (I hated keeping people waiting). I worried that our portions were too small. That our food was too ordinary. That our tea was too weak. Or too strong. Or too something. You get the idea. I stressed about everything, mostly without cause.

I worried that every aspect of the business was not as it should be. And those worries never left me. If anything, they got worse. When customers told me the food was great, I rarely believed them. On the few occasions when customers complained, I outwardly coped magnificently. But inside, I wanted to melt through the floor.

This lack of confidence never left, and I have a suspicion that it is the root cause of our business's demise. It's something that I wish I'd recognised in myself earlier. Because it tells me that I'm more suited to working with ideas than I am to working in a customer-service environment. And I suspect that, if the business owner doesn't suit the environment, the business doesn't stand a chance.

2. Knowing less than the staff

In our business planning, Anne-Maree and I fully expected that we would know less than our staff about the day-to-day operation of a cafe. We aimed to employ experienced cafe staff and we expected they would run the cafe. But we didn't have the financial capacity to employ an experienced cafe manager from day one. Instead, we employed an experienced chef, one experienced barista, and several casuals with cafe experience.

We employed a group of terrific, loyal staff who supported us and worked alongside us to the best of their abilities. Many stayed with us for the full 26 months we were open, and remain friends to this day. But we were all operating in a new environment, with new equipment and emerging procedures. The staff needed us to set the cafe's direction and decide how things would be done. With our limited practical understanding of cafe operation, this proved difficult.

In the early months, Anne-Maree worked three days a week at the university, and I devoted myself full-time to the cafe. I was there every hour the cafe was open. My lack of confidence compounded with my realisation that the staff needed more supervision than I expected.

Even at the time, I understood that buying an existing cafe was preferable to starting a new cafe from scratch. An existing cafe would come with a customer base, trained staff, and operating procedures. I put a lot of effort into searching for an existing cafe that would meet our needs, and failed to find one. Maybe I should have been more patient. Starting from scratch as inexperienced cafe owners was, I believe, a second major cause of our problems.

3. Opinionated customers

I sometimes wonder whether there's something about me that invites other people to tell me what I 'should' be doing. I was dumbfounded by the number of people who came into the shop, either to inspect the venue or to buy from the cafe, and who took it upon themselves to share their opinions about what we needed to do.

In the first weeks of operating this fledgling business, presumably well-meaning people told us that we should: open on Sundays, close on a weekday, pay our staff in cash, forget about regulations, get an alcohol licence, open at night, introduce a breakfast deal, have a better rewards program, keep the newspaper, sell bread and milk, get flashing lights to improve our visibility, install a smartboard, offer video-conferencing equipment, charge more, charge less, offer a membership program, offer the rooms for free, do more letterbox drops, run more events, and so on it went. They're just the ones I remember.

It was a daily assault of unwanted, unsought business advice that did nothing to boost my confidence. Sitting alongside this was a seemingly endless parade of consultants who suggested we engage their services to address some mysterious gap in our business model.

After a few months of this, we banned the word 'should' from our vocabulary. We made our office a 'should-free zone' and agreed that none of the cafe staff would tell the others what they 'should' do. I never fully succeeded in learning to ignore unasked-for advice, but I did learn to take it less seriously.

4. *Few customers*

On paper, our business looked viable. I couldn't have been more prepared or more focused on our financial position. I understood our overheads. I understood our margins. I knew our break-even point in terms of both coffee volume and venue bookings. I understood that coffee volume could balance low venue bookings. I costed our menu items. I always knew our bank balance, and I paid every bill on time.

Every aspect of my planning was spot on, except for one. And it was the one that really mattered.

For some reason that I fail to understand, the expected number of customers never walked through the door. Some days, the cafe and venue were both full, and we could see that the business could be profitable and operate as planned. But most days, our staff were under-employed. And the trouble with a cafe, of course, is it needs to be staffed every day, because you never know when the customers will arrive and you never know which days will be busy.

We did not sit back and wait for customers to turn up. We marketed as aggressively as we could with a low budget. We did letterbox drops, visits to small businesses, newsletters, special offers and events. We were on social media every day. We joined networking groups and I set myself a target of attending at least one networking event every week. We achieved some good coverage in the local media, including a double-page spread in the Sunday newspaper and a spot on commercial television.

Over the 26 months we operated, the cafe gradually increased its turnover. The growth was consistent, but slower than we needed. It was also affected by seasonal variations like holidays and rain. We continued to lose money every week. By the time we closed in May 2018, the cafe was strong enough to support an owner-operator with a reasonable living. But the venue never grew as we anticipated, and we could see that we were not the right people for an owner-operator cafe.

5. Little understanding of the small-business market

In our business planning, we anticipated that the cafe and venue would be used by consultants, researchers, writers, and small-business owners.

We created a cafe space that welcomed people who wanted to spend time working over their coffee and cake. We even had a strategy ready for how we would cope if too many people started to occupy tables for long hours, while only buying one coffee. We also designed our venue packages with small business and consultants in mind. We were confident that our offerings were well priced and fair.

But we quickly discovered that we had little understanding of, and little love for, the wider small-business market. Our university and consulting backgrounds had not prepared us for the ways small-business owners think. The people we initially attracted to the venue were on the lookout for the best deal they could find – the best space and the best food, for the lowest possible price. They had no interest in our business viability.

We found some of our venue customers to be unreasonably demanding and pushy. We encountered many 'business advisors' and 'life coaches' who argued the venue space should be free because they were buying catering. And because we were struggling to build our profile and fill our venue, we often negotiated below the point where it was worthwhile accepting their business. It took many months for us to realise that we were better off having empty rooms than letting the rooms be used by people who didn't generate an income.

Our cafe became a popular meeting venue for distributed businesses (where employees work from their homes or vehicles) to hold their regular staff meetings. At first this seemed like a great asset, and we took many large mid-morning bookings for the cafe. But staff meetings can be long and noisy. They filled the cafe, used our expensive wi-fi, and enjoyed our air-conditioning, often without buying even one drink per person. We were left with a dilemma that was difficult for a fledging business making an ongoing loss: should we set a minimum spend for the cafe, let them know they were only welcome if they booked a room, or perhaps encourage them to go elsewhere?

6. Being all things to all people

Even though I specialise in writing simple words, I have an annoying habit of making most things unnecessarily complex. I get carried away by what is possible, and I end up trying to be all things to all people. In the cafe, it was as though my mantra became: 'sure, we can do that, and perhaps we could also …'.

Over the 26 months that our business operated, in addition to our cafe, gift shop, and venue space, we introduced a monthly games afternoon, a monthly writing event, regular art classes, a monthly philosophy cafe, a small-business advice series, an occasional 'conversations' series, occasional music afternoons, weekly yoga, occasional pop-up events and workshops that we felt people would appreciate, high teas, fancy cakes, external catering, and special functions.

In trying to do too many different things, I believe we fragmented our market and lost our focus. I loved organising events that I thought the local community would enjoy. And I particularly enjoyed organising workshops that interested me and might otherwise not have happened in Brisbane. But each of these required an enormous amount of work and involved a significant level of risk. If we failed to sell enough tickets, the income was negligible. And even though I was usually content the events brought us some promotional benefit, they meant I was working hard for absolutely no income.

7. Not enjoying the day-to-day work

Both Anne-Maree and I know a lot about organising events, and we both enjoy event work. We have jointly and separately organised many, many events, of all shapes and sizes. We had little experience in hospitality, but we'd both worked in food businesses as teenagers and we felt confident enough in our abilities. So, in our planning for the business, it didn't cross our minds that we might not enjoy the day-to-day work of managing a venue and cafe.

I was the one who suffered most. I quickly discovered an active dislike for the extensive work involved in providing quotes, taking bookings, managing enquiries, setting up rooms, and meeting people's requests when they were on site. I became stressed if the meeting room seemed too hot or too cold, if we had trouble with the equipment or, horror of horrors, if we were two minutes late in providing the catering. In most cases, I was stressed about problems that customers didn't even notice.

Anne-Maree coped with this side of the business better than I did. She is more outgoing than me and she enjoys interacting with people. She's very good at anticipating their needs and keeping them happy. But even she found that venue management was extensive work for little reward.

We encountered three ongoing problems with venue management. Firstly, my lack of confidence meant that I kept looking over Anne-Maree's shoulder and sticking my nose in where it wasn't wanted. Secondly, our venue systems were still developing and we didn't have good ways of sharing information between us. Thirdly – and this was the killer for us – managing the venue bookings was more time-consuming than we anticipated, with many fiddly details and difficult requests that made it very difficult for the venue to pay its way.

Behind our decision to close

By the end of 2016, we recognised that we were unlikely to stay in the business for the 10 years we'd originally anticipated. Even though our turnover was growing month by month, we were not breaking even and our cash reserves were worryingly low. The business had taken over every aspect of our lives: our family suffered, our house suffered, our health suffered, and my consulting suffered. The shop was open seven days a week, and we worked very long hours.

For most of 2017, we couldn't see a way to exit. We had 18 months left on the lease, so if our monthly losses were less than the rent, it made sense to continue.

NEWBIES IN THE CAFE

In late-August 2017, we wrote to our customers, letting them know that the business was growing but not yet viable. We asked for their support in building the business. We distributed the letter through the cafe, on social media, and to our 1,000+ newsletter list.

In response to the letter, we were approached by a local drama studio seeking to share our space. Our initial reaction was to say no, because the drama studio wanted to take over the training room – the room that captured our reason for starting the business. But as we thought about it, it started to seem like a way to spread some risk and begin to exit from a business we weren't enjoying.

Following several months of negotiation, we transferred the lease to the drama studio. In December 2017 they took over all the meeting rooms and training room, and we retained the cafe. We became sub-tenants in the building we had renovated, with one year of rent-free access to the cafe and an option to renew for a second year. Even though we had no plans to own the cafe long-term, it seemed like a good way to build the business and make back some of our original investment.

We started 2018 with a simple cafe and much-reduced overheads. But we also found that our customer profile changed. Our small-business customers deserted us, and the drama studio didn't bring in the family customers we'd expected. The cafe didn't thrive, but continued to limp along as an almost-viable business. I reduced my hours in the cafe and began to rebuild my consultancy.

In April 2018, we decided that Anne-Maree should look for a job and we began to explore options for selling the cafe. Our chef was genuinely interested in taking over and we got as far as discussing a price.

But then things happened in quick succession: our chef decided not to purchase a cafe that would have her as sub-tenant to the drama studio, Anne-Maree was offered a full-time job, our barista broke her ankle, and I had a crisis of confidence about working a full week in the kitchen while our chef took leave for her daughter's wedding.

Chapter 2: It helps if you like the work

It was a Saturday in mid-April that we decided we could not continue. We didn't even try to sell the business; as sub-tenants paying no rent, we had no security of tenure, so we didn't really have a business to sell. Instead we traded for another week, selling off whatever we could. Then we closed, dealt with the messy and expensive process of extracting ourselves from our various contracts, found someone who was interested in starting a new cafe in the space, and sold our equipment second hand.

Rediscovering our lives

As I write this case study, it's over a year since we closed the cafe. There's a sense that our family is emerging from trauma and re-learning how to live. We regret the financial hole we dug for ourselves and we regret some of our business decisions. But mostly, we're pleased we gave it a try. We've certainly learned a lot, and we know how to make good coffee.

I'm left dwelling on two questions.

1. Could we have started small and reduced the risk?

When we were planning the business, we were unable to see any way to start small and grow. We saw the complete vision. And because we wanted multiple meeting spaces with a cafe attached, we thought we needed to open everything immediately.

I realise now that it would have been possible to start small and test the idea before taking a huge financial risk. Starting small would have given me an opportunity to learn the critical information I lacked: that I was unlikely to enjoy the day-to-day administration, and that taking bookings for a meetings venue involved extensive work for little return.

What I could have done was rent an office for my consultancy, with enough space to offer a training room for hire. Ideally, the office would have been located next door to a cafe that could provide catering. At the time, that possibility didn't cross my mind. And I'm not sure what mental gymnastics or business advice could have revealed it back in 2012 when it would have been useful.

2. Is it possible to know in advance whether you'll enjoy the work?

One of our big problems was that we didn't enjoy the day-to-day reality of what we were doing. We both loved the idea of a word-themed cafe and a meeting-room venue. We loved the idea of owning it and managing it. We loved telling people about what we were doing, and we were proud of the space we created.

But we were out of our depth. The everyday work wasn't much fun. And my consultant's brain had me primed to set something up and move on. I wasn't prepared for the tedium of implementation and I wasn't willing to put years into work that I didn't much like to achieve a longer-term financial outcome.

I'm not convinced that it's possible to know in advance what the lived experience of any decision will be like. Planning and preparation are important, but they don't tell you what it will be like to actually live through something. My previous experience had led me to believe that most things are easier to do than I expect them to be (for me, completing a PhD sits in that category). So discovering the business was more difficult than I expected and didn't grow as I planned took me by surprise.

Yes, I could have worked in a cafe ahead of time, and I might have learned that I didn't like the work. Yes, I could have worked in a venue. But it would have been easy to rationalise away any negative experiences as being due to the business owner. It's easy to believe that you can do things better yourself.

Would we do it again?

If we knew then what we know now, would we have established the business?

No. And we've no intention of taking the same risks again.

Chapter 2: It helps if you like the work

But if someone had given us an insight into what it would be like, would we have listened? Probably not. This was a journey we needed to take.

Chapter 3

Let the buyer beware!

Newbie: Cheryl Cornish

Cafe: Get Tossed Salad Bar, Albury NSW (2017 –)

Previous occupation: Vocational training and career coaching

Chapter 3: Let the buyer beware!

Cheryl Cornish learned the hard way about the risks of buying a cafe. Just a few weeks after she bought Get Tossed Salad Bar in Albury, NSW, Cheryl discovered the business was not all it seemed to be.

In late 2017, Cheryl became the proud owner of a salad bar–cafe that was well liked by customers, but had a rotten core. She discovered that tradespeople and suppliers didn't want to know her, the premises contravened electrical standards, her equipment was faulty, her website disappeared, and the previous owner's assessments of turnover and profitability seemed inflated, at best.

She calls them 'rookie mistakes' that embarrass her now. And, after 14 months spent solving problems and finding her feet, Cheryl is well on the road to building the business she thought she was buying.

The customer who bought the business

Cheryl's story is a classic tale of the customer who bought the business. It was an unplanned, opportunistic purchase, made at a time when she was looking for change.

'I hadn't been thinking about getting into hospitality,' said Cheryl. 'I knew I wanted a change. I was looking for something different, and this came along. It seemed like the right choice at the time.'

Cheryl was at the tail end of a 15-year career in vocational training and career coaching, mostly in the engineering industry.

'I needed to get out of the industry I was in,' said Cheryl. 'I was burned out and anxious. I needed to leave the corporate environment. But I was having trouble finding another job. I was approaching 60, and I began to think I was invisible and unemployable.

'Then one day, I saw a comment on LinkedIn, saying that Get Tossed was for sale. I thought: I know that place. I love that place! I can cook. This is it!

'I was ripe for an opportunity and, as it turned out, I was ripe for being duped. I remember thinking at the time: I know how to run a business. How hard can it be?

'I know now. The answer is that it can be very, very hard.'

Wearing rose-tinted glasses

Cheryl approached the purchase of her business with enthusiasm and confidence. She wore 'rose-tinted glasses' throughout the negotiation. And she knows she has no one to blame but herself.

'I realise now that I looked at everything through rose-tinted glasses,' she said. 'I saw all the positive sides of the business and ignored all the negatives. I believed everything the previous owner told me. It didn't even cross my mind to do any research that might help me look behind the business and check the accuracy of what I was told.'

Cheryl could see that the shop looked tired and needed a facelift. But she wasn't daunted. On paper, the shop was profitable with a good income for the owner.

'I knew the shop was popular with customers and that people liked the food,' she said. 'I liked the food so that was a good start!'

Cheryl began negotiations with the previous owner in September 2017. Within six weeks, the shop was hers. She worked alongside the previous owner for two weeks, and then she was on her own.

'The previous owner would have preferred to sell for cash, on a handshake,' she said. 'I insisted on a proper contract, checked by solicitors. I'm so glad I did that step at least, because it meant we had a solid agreement with some clear conditions.

'But as a rookie, I assumed the seller's solicitor would do due diligence to check the financial reporting was accurate. And that wasn't the case. No one ever checked whether the paperwork was an accurate record. And I didn't think to do any research about the business and the way it was run.'

A pathway to retirement

Cheryl imagined that Get Tossed would be her pathway to retirement. She used a lump sum from her superannuation to fund her purchase. Her plan was to work as owner-manager for four or five years, build the turnover, improve the profitability, and then sell.

Chapter 3: Let the buyer beware!

At the time of our conversation, Cheryl was 14 months into that journey. She's still on the same path, but the journey has been more difficult than expected. And her hopes for a reasonable income have been dashed. After 14 months, she's yet to take an income, and she's yet to break even.

Dream vs. reality

Just before Christmas 2017, a few weeks after she took over Get Tossed, Cheryl started to smell a rat, both literal and metaphorical.

Not only did the shop need renovation and equipment repair, the difficulties started to pile up. Her dream of a simple life in hospitality died and the hard work began.

Cheryl's first problem was that the shop's website – its main promotional tool – disappeared overnight. Cheryl discovered that its hosting was based on a contra deal: hosting in return for coffee. When the previous owner left, the website went with him. Cheryl needed to build a new website from scratch, putting her on a steep learning curve and interrupting her supposedly seamless takeover.

Cheryl's second problem was finding tradespeople and suppliers. 'Tradespeople wouldn't work for me, and suppliers wouldn't let me open accounts. I discovered that the shop had a terrible reputation in the industry for slow payment and bad debt. I'd get off the phone in tears, after begging people to do the work we needed. I had to persuade people that "new Get Tossed" wasn't the same as "old Get Tossed". It took me months of hard work and stress.'

Cheryl's most significant problem was electrical, discovered following a small fire in the kitchen just two months after she bought the business. An electrician refused to repair the damage because the shop had no standard safety switches and an incorrectly located switchboard.

'Basically we were in a non-compliant building,' said Cheryl. 'Even though the building owner did the repairs we needed, it was a negotiation I could have done without.

'My mistake wasn't so much that I bought a shop with problems. It's that I should have known about all these problems before I bought. If I'd known about the problems, I could have negotiated appropriately. But I was naive, and I didn't think to ask.

'When I look back now, I'm embarrassed by the rookie mistakes I made. I shudder when I remember laughing with the previous owner about the condition of the equipment. Instead of laughing, I should have negotiated.'

Understanding commercial leasing

When she was buying the business, Cheryl paid little attention to the commercial lease.

'The lease was there, but I didn't give much thought to it,' she said. 'I just assumed it was a standard lease, with nothing much to concern me. I didn't think about how different a commercial lease is from a residential lease.'

Cheryl was interviewed by the building owner, so that he could confirm she was a suitable tenant for his building. But it didn't cross her mind to interview him in return.

'When I think back now, I'm astonished that I went into a commercial lease so lightly,' said Cheryl. 'When people buy houses, they're so careful about things like building inspections and title searches. Commercial leasing should be the same.

'Commercial leasing was a whole new game for me. I had no idea that I would be responsible for everything. I should have understood it more fully. I didn't even think to investigate it. That was another one of my rookie mistakes.'

Doing the right thing by staff

When Cheryl bought Get Tossed, she was determined to do the right thing by her staff, with fair pay and fair employment conditions. She hadn't anticipated it would be a challenging commitment.

Chapter 3: Let the buyer beware!

'In this industry, many people are paid in cash,' she said. 'A lot of hospitality workers don't get paid properly and don't get their superannuation.

'Paying people properly and carrying the right insurances are huge expenses. But they matter. If I can't employ people fairly, I shouldn't be in business. I employ mostly permanent staff, not casuals. I pay award wages. I pay super. I'm fully insured. And all those things make it harder for me to break even.

'The benefit for me is that my staff turnover is very low and my staff are loyal. Another big benefit is that I can take advantage of government incentives for employers. But I feel that it's hard to compete, because so many people in the industry don't follow the rules.

'I'd really like to see some type of "fair work tick" so that customers know which businesses pay staff properly and which businesses don't. I'd like to find a way of promoting that I do the right thing.'

The coffee matters

Get Tossed is a salad bar, selling a variety of salads, meats, rolls, wraps, and simple sweet treats. Since buying the business, Cheryl has added baked potatoes and seasonal soup to the menu.

For Cheryl, Get Tossed is a food business, with coffee and cold drinks as a sideline. But she quickly discovered that coffee could make or break the business.

'I didn't realise that I was buying a coffee business,' she said. 'I thought the coffee was less important. But I quickly discovered that good coffee is absolutely vital. People demand it.'

Cheryl invested in a new grinder, learned a lot about coffee, and started to buy beans from a local roaster. It's been a popular move that has helped her build the business.

Paying for advice

In her first year as a cafe owner, Cheryl paid a marketing consultant to help with promotion. Together, they developed the business's social media presence, introduced a loyalty scheme, and launched an online ordering system.

'I needed to learn about social media and learn how to promote the business locally,' she said. 'Working with a consultant helped to build my confidence, which I really needed. And the consultant also helped to build the business's profile more quickly than I could have done alone.

Investing in the marketing consultant was a great move for my first year, but now I feel I'm ready to do it myself.'

For her second year in the business, Cheryl plans to invest in a business advisor.

'I feel that I spent the first year learning how to run the business,' she said. 'I implemented a lot of new systems, including a proper accounting system and a point of sale. Now that I'm getting proper data about the business, it's time to work with someone who can help me build it.

'My goal is to break even this year and begin to take an income. And I realise now that I need good advice to achieve it.'

Trying to make a difference

Cheryl is slowly transforming Get Tossed into a business that supports her ways of viewing the world.

'I'm trying to do my bit to support local businesses,' said Cheryl. 'I think it's particularly important for small local businesses to support each other. I buy local meat, local bread, local sweets, and locally roasted coffee, all from small businesses. And I've joined the Chamber of Commerce so that I can be part of a business network for local businesses.'

Cheryl also believes that businesses should do their part to support environmental initiatives. When she first took over the business, Cheryl introduced recyclable and low-waste packaging. Now she's turned her attention to green waste.

Chapter 3: Let the buyer beware!

'We produce a huge amount of green waste in the hospitality industry,' said Cheryl. 'There's currently no local program to help us compost that waste. We have domestic green-waste collection in Albury, but nothing for businesses. And it's businesses that produce the biggest volume of waste.'

Cheryl has started to provide her green waste to a local gardener, who turns it into compost. In return, the gardener provides Get Tossed with fresh herbs and tomatoes.

'In three months, I provided 340 kilograms of green waste to be made into compost,' said Cheryl. 'That's a huge amount of waste that would otherwise end up in landfill, that's now been turned into useful compost.

'It's easy enough for me to do it because I can work with my friend who has a garden. But think of the difference we could make if we had an industry-wide composting scheme. I'd love to see the local councils take action on this.'

Cheryl is pragmatic about her environmental efforts and the benefits it brings for her business.

'It's important to me that I support environmental initiatives because I believe we need to take steps to reduce our environmental footprint,' she said. 'But I can also see that it brings benefits to the shop. Customers like to know that we're trying to do the right thing. It's a good promotional tool as well as being something that benefits the environment.'

Working on the business, not in it

Cheryl estimates that she works 10 hours in the shop each day, with an additional two hours at home most nights. The saving grace is that the shop only opens five days a week.

'Until now, I've worked in the shop every day it's been open,' said Cheryl. 'This year, I plan to try staying away for two mornings each week, so that I can work *on* the business not *in* the business. I've introduced a supervisor role, so that I can be away from the shop. Now I just need to make it happen.'

Cheryl has been surprised by how much hands-on work she does in the shop every day.

'I didn't realise that staff need so much supervision and support,' she said. 'I often fall into the trap of thinking it's easier to do things myself. But if I'm going to grow the business and get some balance for myself, I need to learn to step back and let the staff take more responsibility.'

Not what she expected

Cheryl readily admits that the salad bar business is nothing like she expected it to be. It's harder than she expected, with longer hours, more hands-on work, and an unpredictable income.

'Some days, I feel like I'm living inside an episode of *I'm a Celebrity … Get me out of here!*,' said Cheryl. 'It's such hard work. I had no idea it would be so hard. Even putting aside the mistakes I made when I bought the business, it's harder than I expected.'

Financially, the business is nothing like Cheryl expected. 'On paper, it looked like the shop was making a profit,' she said. 'But my experience is so different from those original figures. The turnover isn't as high as I expected it to be, and the expenses are bigger.

'The unexpected expenses for repairs and new equipment have made me feel the pinch financially. I really thought I'd be able to earn an income straight away. But we've ended up going into a bit of debt and we're not quite breaking even yet. I can see that it's getting better, but it's slower than I expected.'

Cheryl is also surprised by what she describes as the 'unpredictability' of the hospitality industry.

'I always thought that cafes had a stable pattern of busy times and quiet times,' she said. 'But no one can predict what days and times will be busy. Everyone thinks they know, and everyone thinks they can explain the trends. But they're really just guessing and looking for excuses.

'For the first 12 months I tried to predict people's behaviour, and it just made me question my judgement. Now I'm beginning to learn that it can't be predicted. I'm learning to accept that.'

Embarrassed by her mistakes

When Cheryl looks back over her first 14 months in business, she's embarrassed by some of her mistakes but confident she can continue.

'There's so much that I should have done before buying the business,' said Cheryl. 'I should have done more research. I should have learned more about hospitality. I should have negotiated harder. I should have taken off those damn rose-tinted glasses!

'But I didn't, and I've paid for it. I was so naive. For the first six months, I kept thinking: *What have I done? Why have I bought this business?*

'But after six months I started to feel better, and now I'm feeling much more confident about the future.

'I feel that Get Tossed is well on the way to building a strong, positive reputation. It was always reasonably popular with customers, and I've been able to build on that strength. I've also been able to build new, positive relationships with suppliers and tradespeople.'

And, on the positive side, Cheryl has discovered a love for hospitality.

'I really like the work I'm doing. I love the customer side of it.

'I left the corporate world because I was anxious and burned out. This place takes my anxiety away. Maybe it's because I'm so busy that I don't have time to be anxious! But making good food and having satisfied customers is a good feeling.'

Chapter 4

Dream big, work hard, love the work

Newbie: Alex Milosovic

Cafe: Extraction Artisan Coffee, Slacks Creek Qld (2016 –)

Previous occupation: Steel fabricator

Chapter 4: Dream big, work hard, love the work

Alex Milosevic closed a successful steel fabrication business to follow his dream of opening Logan City's first artisan coffee roastery and cafe. In April 2016, his vision became a reality when he opened Extraction Artisan Coffee in Slacks Creek, an industrial part of Logan, about 30 km south of Brisbane.

Extraction's tagline? #gratitude

Alex worked in steel fabrication for 28 years. For the last 12 of those years, he operated the business after his father retired. 'I really enjoyed steel fabrication,' said Alex. 'But after the global turndown, things got hard. I was tired, and I guess I was bored.'

Just as he was tiring of steel fabrication, Alex discovered coffee. 'I discovered coffee in a big way,' said Alex. 'For years I'd loved wine. I wasn't any great expert, but I kept about 400 bottles in my cellar at home. Then I discovered that coffee is just as complex as wine. There's so much to it.

'I learned more, and an old friend started pestering me about joining his coffee roasting business. I put him off for a long time because I already had a business. But eventually I thought, *Bugger it. I'm 50 years old. I've got to do something now or I won't ever do it.* So I closed the steel business and went into coffee. That's how it all started.'

Alex worked at his friend's roastery for more than two years, learning the trade. But eventually he got tired of the long days working in someone else's business. He decided to go out on his own.

'The industry sucked me in,' said Alex. 'I can see now that I probably should have been doing this for the last 35 years. I was a good steel fabricator and I enjoyed it. The skills I learned from steel really helped me start this business. But this is what I love.'

Alex's dream business

In 2014, Alex and his wife Heather started to dream about owning their own coffee business. Some good friends had been toying with

45

the idea of opening a cafe, so the two couples decided to start a venture together.

'Back then we didn't know how we'd find the money,' said Alex. 'We just decided to do whatever we could to get it going. We decided to get as far as we could and if we got stuck we'd figure out what to do next.

'One of the main reasons I wanted to start the business was because there was nowhere between Brisbane and the Gold Coast where I could buy specialty coffee. There was no one roasting here and I thought Logan was the perfect location.'

The first step was finding the right premises. Alex and Heather decided to set up their own superannuation fund and buy premises for their business. It took some months to find the right location.

'We looked at buildings for three or four months and couldn't find anything to suit us. I knew about a warehouse in Slacks Creek – the building we ended up buying. I'd dismissed it without even looking inside, because it didn't look suitable at all.

'An agent convinced me to look inside, and the minute I came into the building I knew that it could actually work. It was full of old equipment from yarn dying – pallets and racks and boilers and ovens – but I could see it would work for us. It had the right feel and the right space.

'So we bought it and the business pays rent to our superannuation fund. I was confident that buying the building was the best way for us to go. It's an asset. If the coffee business didn't work I could always buy a bench and set up a steel business here. Or we could sell it if necessary. It was definitely the right move for us.

'People often ask me why we bought a building in the back of an industrial estate, with no street frontage and very little signage. It's not an obvious place for a cafe. But we knew that people would come here because they'd heard about us, not because of our location. If we got it right, they would want to come and want to come back, so our location didn't matter.'

Chapter 2: Dream big, work hard, love the work

Turning the dream into a reality

It took around 12 months from the day Alex and Heather bought the building to the day they finally opened the doors.

'We had to go through all the rigmarole of getting council approval for the renovation and fitout,' said Alex. 'We were putting a coffee business into an industrial warehouse. It took a lot of negotiation. I learned that when people came to inspect the building, they would all read the situation a little differently. I also discovered that inspectors don't sign off on things, regardless of the discussions we had. So I started going into council to talk with the person who made the decisions. I was always very respectful, but I learned to take my questions directly to the decision makers.

'My business experience helped a lot. Because I had experience, I wasn't afraid to ask questions. Business is business, and even if the product changes, there are some simple guidelines about how businesses have to operate. Common sense and business knowledge helped me to argue my case.

'I'm a business person first. Even today I'm not a barista or a coffee roaster. I'm a businessman. I can make a pretty decent coffee. I can run the till and clean the tables and wash the dishes. I can do every job here except run the kitchen. But I'm a businessman and that's my focus.'

Finding the funds for the fitout

Alex and Heather were short of the funds needed to make their dream a reality. They spent a lot of time seeking a bank loan, without any success.

'We were knocked back by four or five banks,' said Alex. 'We were looking for an unsecured loan, and it was too risky. Each bank took a long time to make their decision, and it wasted a lot of our time.

'I wondered about setting up a welding shop for a year and earning the money that way. But eventually we decided to sell our house to fund the business. We had enough equity in the house to do most of the fitout, and I did a lot of the work myself.

'Heather has a small graphic design business, and she continued to operate that. She's kept the graphic design business to this day, operating from the cafe's office. While we were doing the business planning, I worked as a casual at Myer to earn enough money to keep us afloat.'

When the fitout was almost complete, Alex and Heather once again ran short of money. 'We were stuck,' said Alex. 'The fitout was pretty much done, and we'd bought our roaster. But we couldn't afford to buy a coffee machine and grinder. And we couldn't afford our first batch of coffee beans. We needed about $25,000.

'Heather had the idea of trying crowdfunding. She set up a fundraising page and we offered little benefits like t-shirts, coffee from our first batch, and attending our opening party. And it worked!

'We had some amazing friends who helped us out. They really wanted us to succeed. It makes me emotional now to think those people put so much faith and trust in us. It made us want to succeed for them. We didn't want to let them down.'

Alex and Heather bought their coffee machine and set their opening date: 23 April 2016. They also borrowed $35,000 from private lenders to give them operating capital for the first few months.

'That $35,000 was essential,' said Alex. 'It meant we knew we could pay the wages and the immediate expenses in those early days. Thankfully we got busy quickly and we were able to pay it off.'

With the doors open, Alex and Heather's dream had become a reality.

Business planning

Alex and Heather developed a detailed business plan with conservative estimates of their potential income.

'A lot of people in the industry thought we were being too conservative in our planning,' said Alex. 'They all thought we could do better than we'd put in the plan. But we were using the business plan to apply for loans, so we thought it made sense to be conservative.

'The business plan was a real help in getting us started. And we were very lucky. We probably wouldn't have done it if we hadn't been given some help.

'We have a friend who is an accountant in a large firm. They'd decided to open a business advice section, helping people do business plans. And they wanted to develop a template. So I spent time with them, talking about what we were doing, formulating our business plan, and helping them develop their template.

'We didn't pay a cent for it because it was their business development. And here's the thing: I probably couldn't have paid for it, because we didn't have the money. But it certainly would have been worth paying for. Hindsight is a wonderful thing.

'I'm happy with the planning we did before we opened and I think it really helped us get started, but it would have helped if I'd known more about how to operate a kitchen. Running the kitchen has been the hardest part of this business.'

Business promotion

Alex and Heather understood from the beginning that they would need a lot of promotion to bring people to their business. They set about creating a community of supporters who wanted to see them succeed. Heather put a lot of time into social media promotion. She shared their journey, right down to frank discussions about the sale of their house.

'By the time we opened, we had over 700 followers on Facebook,' said Alex. 'People were really interested in what we were doing. We've been open nearly three-and-a-half years now, and we've got close to 5,250 followers on Facebook and over 3,850 on Instagram. It's been a slow climb and a lot of work, but the social media profile gives us a lot of credibility as a business.'

Alex and Heather also put a lot of thought into developing a brand that would work well for them. Heather's experience as a graphic designer helped them to capture an image that reflected their business purpose and community-based approach.

'A lot of people sell coffee and food,' said Alex. 'And it can be great coffee and great food. But if people don't like you, if they don't like your staff, or if they don't like the energy when they walk in, they're not going to come back.'

As part of their promotion, Alex and Heather have built a strong relationship with the Logan City Council. 'We're very focused on the community and supportive of our city,' said Alex. 'You hear a lot of bad things about Logan, and you rarely hear the good things. I think we're one of the most diverse cities on the planet. We've got 237 different nationalities living here and it's amazing.

'So Extraction is all about Logan and what this city has to offer. And when the council wants to market the city, we're their biggest advocate. That's how we ended up getting a visit from Ainsley Harriet this year, for the SBS documentary series he's making.'

The business partnership

Extraction was originally started as a two-couple partnership, with Alex and Heather in partnership with friends. Alex and Heather developed the business and funded the fitout, but the plan was for joint operation of the business.

'We're great mates,' said Alex. 'My friend worked here for about three months when we first opened. But we operate very differently. And we didn't like working together.

'Thankfully we had an exit strategy. We decided to sort it out, and we got an independent mediator in to help us. We needed someone who wasn't emotionally invested in either of us.

'Having a mediator was good. She kept saying *I understand what you're saying, but why are you feeling that? What's the underlying cause?* We discovered that some of our values lined up, but a lot of them

Chapter 4: Dream big, work hard, love the work

didn't. And I realised that the other couple didn't want to spend long hours working here. They've got grandchildren, and wanted to spend time with their family. And I was entirely focused on what we needed to do for the business.

'It took some time, but we all came around to the idea that it wasn't going to work for us to be in the business together. Then my friend offered to do all our paperwork – all the payroll, all the invoices, everything. We're three years in, and he still does that for us. And he does it for free.

'He's here every day and he does it for coffee and for love. It says something about the ethic and the energy of what we do here.'

Long hours for little income

Extraction is open seven days a week, and Alex works every day. For Alex, it's an essential investment in the success of his business.

'I'm the front face of the business, and I spend a lot of time working on the coffee machine,' said Alex. 'But I can see that I need to get away from it more. I need to start working on the business, rather than in it. We're just getting to the point now where it can operate without me and I can change my focus.'

After three years of hard work, Alex and Heather are able to draw a small wage from Extraction. 'It's a big drop in income from what we used to earn,' said Alex. 'But we're still living. We still eat. We're probably not as rested as we'd like and we haven't had a proper break in three years. But we're doing OK.

'I don't put a lot of value on material things. I really value people. And that's what is making this business a success. We value every person who comes through the door. If you're a complete stranger and you want to buy a cup of coffee here, I'm going to treat you the same as I treat my best friend. Because that will bring you back.'

Understanding competition

When Alex and Heather started to develop their ideas for Extraction, they had little competition in Logan City. That's changed, with several independent cafes now operating nearby. But Alex is convinced that competition is positive.

'If someone opened another cafe next door, and they had a really good roast and they did crazy good food, that should just inspire me to be better. To have better style. To offer what people want.

'When you're in business, the only person you really compete against is yourself. It's your attitude that matters. You need to have the right attitude for the community.'

Trusting staff and suppliers

Alex's approach to life is based on trust. 'I only work with people I trust and I believe that people trust me to be honest,' said Alex. 'There are times when I've been disappointed by people, but usually the trust pays off.

'Because of the way I think, I don't hire staff based on their skills. I'm interested in whether I can trust them and what they're like as people. When we interview new staff, we don't ask them to use the coffee machine. We don't ask them to show us what they can do. We just ask them to tell us who they are. I can teach staff how to pour coffee and how to sweep the floor. But I can't teach personality.

'If staff show us they're loyal to the business, we prefer to have them as permanent staff, not casuals. Being permanent gives them security. They know what's happening next week. They know they're getting holidays. I have an obligation to them, but I get loyalty from them. That's the way I work with staff who give back to us, who treat this business like it's their own business.

'Maybe the staff trust me because I'm a team player. If they're busy in the cafe, I jump in. I wash dishes. I clean up. I sweep floors. We're a team. They only succeed if we succeed.'

Chapter 4: Dream big, work hard, love the work

Alex's advice to others

Alex and Heather have no regrets about starting Extraction, and they'd recommend it for anyone with a passion for the coffee business. But people need to know what they're letting themselves in for.

'I'd say that if you're prepared to work harder than you've ever worked before, for less than you've ever earned, for at least the next three to five years, with absolutely no guarantee of seeing a financial return from it, then go for it,' said Alex.

'I'd also say that if you want to have some of the greatest experiences possible, develop the best relationships you've ever had, learn things about yourself you never knew, and learn about other people's stories, then this is the right business for you.

'And if you want to work in a place that's different every day – even though the tasks are the same, it's different because the people are different – then you'll love this business.

'People buy into the romance of what a cafe is and what it can be. But it's a lot of hard work. If it wasn't for your customers, you wouldn't stay in it. One of the reasons I come to work every day is because there are customers I really love.

'Pride brings me back too. I'm not going to fail. I'm going to succeed at this.

'I think it's good to have a fallback. Because I've got a fallback skill, I'm confident enough to take the risk. But I'm also fairly confident that I'll succeed. I'm determined. Right now, this business is on the edge of being successful. Once that happens we're going to invest back into it to secure it for future years.

'You only get out of life what you put into it. If you're going to wait for someone to hand you stuff, that's fine. But I've personally never waited for someone to give me something.'

Chapter 5

A four-year foray into the coffee shop world

Newbie: Jen Robertson and Terri Kerr

Cafe: Giggles, Jindalee Qld (1995 – 1999)

Previous occupation: Retail and administration

Chapter 5: A four-year foray into the coffee shop world

Sisters Jen Robertson and Terri Kerr and their cousin Vicki Ozorio are long-time foodies who followed their dreams and opened a cafe in Brisbane's western suburbs. In 1995, they opened Giggles, in Jindalee. They sold four-and-a-half years later.

They had some great experiences, with lots of ups and downs. But by the end they were exhausted, with not a lot of financial reward to show for their hard work.

The dream

Before the cafe, Jen worked in retail for many years. She was ready for something new. Terri was working part-time in administration while raising two young children. Vicki was commuting between Hong Kong and Brisbane.

They'd talked on and off over the years about opening a cafe. Jen and Terri both loved cooking, and they were all passionate about food. They were often disappointed with the cafes they visited. 'The food always seemed the same,' said Jen. 'There was very little quality homemade food available in Brisbane at the time. It was the idea of selling great food that captured us most.'

Terri was inspired by a new cafe that opened near her office in Brisbane. 'I was working in advertising administration, and a new cafe opened nearby,' said Terri. 'It inspired me to follow my dream of cooking. I wanted to create a happy, relaxed environment where people could come together and share good, home-cooked food.

'I got caught up in the dream of having a place just like it. I thought it would be so much fun. We both thought that owning a cafe would be exciting. We both love food and love spending time with people. We thought we could make it work.'

Ready for a new opportunity

In the mid-1990s, Jen and Terri were both looking for a new opportunity. It was Terri's husband who finally gave them the push. 'Jen

NEWBIES IN THE CAFE

and I talked about opening a coffee shop on and off for a couple of years,' said Terri. 'One day my husband said that we should just go for it. He gave us the incentive we needed. He encouraged us to get serious about the planning. Vicki was a huge fan of our cooking, so the three of us formed a partnership.'

Jen, Terri, and Vicki chose the name Giggles because it captured the essence of who they are. 'We're notorious for our family laugh,' said Terri. 'We all have happy dispositions, and we love to have a good laugh. Sometimes when we had Giggles, customers would ask us about the name. But they soon figured it out. There was a lot of laughing in the cafe.'

Private investment

As Jen and Terri couldn't back the business financially, they approached Vicki to be a partner and financial backer.

'Vicki loved the idea of co-owning a cafe with us and thought we'd do really well with our cooking skills,' said Jen. 'She gave us the financial support we needed to create our dream. Without her, Giggles would never have happened.

'Vicki divides her time between Hong Kong and Australia. She was spending a lot of time in Hong Kong back then. Whenever she was in Australia, she was fully involved in the cafe. She brought lots of enthusiasm. She loved decorating and adding her ideas to the place. And she loved to bring in her friends to try all our delicious goodies. She loved our food and the atmosphere we created.'

Naive and inexperienced

When they reflect on Giggles, Jen and Terri agree their lack of experience in hospitality made things more difficult than they needed to be.

'There was so much to learn,' said Terri. 'We were confident about the cooking, but we had to learn every other aspect of the business. The whole experience was a learning curve, and we made a few rookie mistakes along the way.'

Chapter 5: A four-year foray into the coffee shop world

'We knew what was needed to get set up, but it was a whole new world for us,' said Jen. 'Although we did a business plan, we lacked experience. We were amateurs, learning as we went along. And wow did we learn along the way!

'We bought a meat slicer, and that's an example of one of our mistakes. We decided to buy at auction. But due to our lack of auction experience we paid a lot more then we needed to. There was a fly buzzing around Terri's head, and swatting the fly drove up the price! It was an Italian slicer and we had all sorts of trouble cleaning it. Eventually, we threw it away, writing it off as a poor purchase.'

Fitting out an empty shop

The three women leased an empty shop in Jindalee, in a small, busy shopping centre with a bakery, newsagent, real estate agent, florist, and hairdresser.

'We scouted around and felt that the demographic and location of Jindalee made it a good location,' said Terri. 'The local community was incredibly supportive. But we really needed more passing trade. In hindsight, we can see that the location could have been better.'

They fitted out the shop from scratch, which they think probably cost them more than buying an existing business. But there weren't many established cafes on the market back then.

'We employed a cabinet maker to do the work and bought brand new display cabinets,' said Jen. 'If we'd had more experience, we probably would have made some different decisions. We could have bought more suitable equipment. If we were doing it again today, we'd buy an existing cafe that was already fully equipped.'

Sharing the load

Jen and Terri were both hands-on in the cafe. They shared the work and divided the hours between them. They both served customers, cooked the food, placed orders, and cleaned. They shared the job of collecting Terri's children from school. Terri did the shop's bookwork and administration.

'I think we both felt a bit guilty that the other one was doing more,' said Jen. 'It was actually a very fair division of tasks. Terri could do the accounts from home, which was great for her as she had young kids. I spent a bit more time in the cafe. We planned and cooked together. Terri's speciality was cakes and I loved the savoury side.'

Strong growth, poor income

Giggles quickly became a busy cafe, popular with the local community. 'We responded to a real need in the community,' said Jen. 'The locals loved Giggles and we established a very strong, regular clientele.'

But even though they were busy, Giggles didn't ever bring in the income they had anticipated.

'We were able to draw a small income from the early days,' said Jen. 'But it was hard, heavy work, and long hours. We could have earned more working for an employer. Basically, we worked very long hours for very little income.'

Extended hours

In their third year of operation, Jen, Terri, and Vicki decided to open Giggles in the evenings, for dinner. They were responding to customer requests for night-time trade. They employed a chef and extended their menu.

'Employing the chef was a big move for us,' said Jen. 'It was a huge risk. And for quite a long time, it was a success. We had some fabulous times when things were running really smoothly and our families enjoyed being at Giggles with our customers.

'We enjoyed great success for about two years. But unfortunately things soured, and we were put in a position where we frequently needed to hire casual agency chefs for the night service. It was a disaster.

'The agency chefs weren't always reliable in providing what we expected, and it's wasn't always possible for us to be there to monitor the situation. We felt the quality of our food suffered and we lost customers because of the inconsistency.

'It was a stressful time. We'd put a lot of work into building our reputation, and we could see it starting to fall apart. We could also see it was starting to cause rifts between us, and we decided it wasn't worth it.'

Trouble with the margins

Giggles always had trouble achieving a profit margin with food sales. 'We didn't skimp on our ingredients,' said Jen.

'We made top-quality food with excellent ingredients. We felt we were buying wisely, but we didn't ever skimp on the quality. To us, quality and consistency were critical. We knew that some customers thought our prices were a bit high for the suburbs. They wanted our style of food, but they didn't want to pay premium prices.

'Every week we struggled to make ends meet, while working very long hours. Vicki supported us financially and always believed in us.'

Struggling financially

Financially, Giggles was always difficult. 'We never seemed to be making any money,' said Terri. 'We always seemed to be saving up to cover some expense.

'I remember one time we'd saved to re-stock the drinks fridge. We had a new casual working with us, and we got her to stack the precious drinks into the fridge. And somehow, we still don't know how it happened, the drinks all fell out. It was like a domino effect, with each shelf collapsing onto each other.

'The noise was incredible, the poor girl was mortified, and we all just stood there in shock. Eventually we started laughing. What else can you do? And then we discovered how hard it is to clean soft drink off the floor. In the process we created some kind of soft-drink glue. After hours of trying to get the floor back to normal, we were back where we started: without drinks in the fridge.'

There were a number of times when they struggled to cover their rent. 'Rent was a killer,' said Terri. 'Near the end, I approached the landlord and asked for some leniency. I had my speech all planned in advance.

'I explained how we were really struggling, what tactics we had in place, and pointed out how much business we had brought into the centre. He wasn't forthcoming at first, but I surprised myself by staying strong and determined. Eventually he relented with some free rent.

'But an expense like the rent is never going to go away. The landlord has to be paid.'

Recognising exhaustion

The long opening hours became an increasing problem for Jen and Terri. 'We were exhausted all the time,' said Jen. 'When everyone else was going home tired after a day's work, we'd be turning around to clean the cafe. We were on our feet all day. There was never a moment to sit down.

'Even when we finally went home at night, we couldn't leave the cafe behind. There was still paperwork to do. We were still worried about how to make it a success. We thought about it constantly.'

Jen and Terri both reached a point where they couldn't keep going. 'I felt like it consumed our every moment,' said Terri. 'I felt guilty about not spending time with my children, and I just didn't want to keep going.'

'We were so tired,' said Jen. 'It was a six-day-a-week business, we were both working extremely hard, and we never had a real break. We were over it.'

Years later, Terri asked her children about the experience. 'I asked them whether they hated the cafe and the time I spent there,'

Chapter 5: A four-year foray into the coffee shop world

said Terri. 'They told me they loved it and wished we hadn't closed. My daughter said she would even love a cafe of her own!'

Jen, Terri, and Vicki sold Giggles within six months of putting it up for sale.

Moving on, without regrets

After Giggles sold, Jen and Terry were exhausted, relieved, and in need of a break.

'We discovered the world had changed since we'd last been employed,' said Jen. 'I wanted to find a job where I wouldn't be on my feet all day, so I didn't want to return to retail. And that meant I needed to re-train. I started with a computer course, and went from there. We both ended up with good jobs in a recruitment company.'

The sisters say they have no regrets about Giggles, but they've got no plans to return to cafe life.

'We had a lot of fun, and we learned a lot,' said Jen. 'But we were exhausted. We had reached our limit and we could see that we were never going to get rich doing this.

'It was a great experience, and we're glad we did it. But we'd had enough.'

But even 10 years later, they were remembered by locals. 'It was a highlight for us,' said Terri. 'Even 10 years after we closed, locals still stopped us and asked when we were opening again because they missed Giggles. That made it all worthwhile!'

Advice to others

Jen and Terri often find themselves talking to people who dream of opening a cafe. Jen offers three pieces of advice:

1. Own the shop. 'I think it makes good sense to own the shop outright,' said Jen. 'Paying a landlord is such a waste of money. I think people have a much better chance of success if they own the shop.'

2. Buy an existing cafe. 'It's better to buy an existing cafe, preferably a closed one as it's more likely to be cheap,' said Jen. 'Buying an existing cafe is so much cheaper than starting from scratch. And you get the benefit of seeing how someone else has operated. We started with an empty shell, and we think it was a big mistake.'

3. Get a liquor licence. 'I think it's hard to make money without a liquor licence,' said Jen. 'I'm sure that being licensed would have made a big difference to us. Particularly once we were open at night for dinner, having a liquor licence would have helped a lot.'

Northside Meetings with The Letter Lounge Cafe & Gifts logo

The courtyard garden at The Letter Lounge, with book mural painted by Anne-Maree Jaggs (Photo: Judy Gregory)

Front entrance to The Letter Lounge in Brisbane's Red Hill (Photo: Judy Gregory)

High tea at The Letter Lounge – complete with paper flowers and quotes about coffee and tea (Photo: Judy Gregory)

Inside The Letter Lounge Cafe, with staff member Freyja Phillips modelling a Storiarts scarf (Photo: Judy Gregory)

Word-themed gifts at The Letter Lounge (Photo: Judy Gregory)

Cheryl Cornish at the entrance to Get Tossed Salad Bar in Albury (Photo: Get Tossed staff member Georgie Springer)

Cheryl Cornish enjoying a quiet moment in the outdoor seating area at Get Tossed Salad Bar (Photo: Get Tossed staff member Georgie Springer)

Alex Milosovic and his wife Heather Scott, proud owners of Extraction Artisan Coffee in Logan (Photo: Stuart Shepherd, One Universe Studio)

Inside Alex Milosovic's cafe Extraction Artisan Coffee in Logan City (Photo: Stuart Shepherd, One Universe Studio)

The team at Cow Cow displaying L-plates on the cafe's opening day; Far right: Anne Roussac-Hoyne; Third from right: Sharni (Photo: Cafe well-wisher)

Inside Anne Roussac-Hoyne's cafe Cow Cow, with Sharni making coffee for a customer (Photo: Cow Cow staff)

Anne Roussac-Hoyne, camera shy outside the entrance to Cow Cow in Foster (Photo: Cow Cow staff)

Chapter 6

The accidental cafe

Newbie: Anne Roussac-Hoyne

Cafe: Cow Cow, Foster Vic (2018 –)

Previous occupation: French teacher, gallery owner, editor, artist

NEWBIES IN THE CAFE

Anne Roussac-Hoyne didn't set out to open a cafe. But what choice did she have?

Anne owns YEPgallery, a thriving art gallery in Foster, near Wilsons Promontory in country Victoria. Her gallery's busiest days are Saturdays and Sundays, when Foster's two cafes are closed.

So Anne opened Cow Cow in late 2018 – a cosy, French-inspired, artistic cafe offering locally roasted coffee and simple, home-style food.

Cow Cow is more an opportune accident than a planned dream. But it's an accident Anne is embracing with characteristic enthusiasm and charm.

'I didn't ever dream about opening a cafe,' said Anne. 'But gallery visitors often asked us to recommend a local cafe. And on weekends there was nowhere.

'Foster is a tourist area and we get a lot of visitors from Melbourne. I thought that maybe the gallery and the cafe would support each other and bring more people to town.

'I love food and I love people, so opening a cafe seemed like an easy decision.'

A retirement portfolio career

Anne is a retired French teacher – a self-described Francophile who loves to bring a French flair to everything she does. She's also an energetic go-getter who sees retirement as an opportunity to try out new things.

'I'm officially retired, but I've always had heaps of energy,' said Anne. 'These days, I do things because I want to – because they seem like a good idea and because I think I'll enjoy them. If they stop being fun, I'll pull the plug on them.'

Anne's approach to life gives her a portfolio career that most people would find breathtaking (or exhausting). In addition to the cafe and gallery, Anne is a French examiner with the Victorian Curriculum and Assessment Authority, an editor, an artist, and a soon-to-be bakery owner.

Chapter 6: The accidental cafe

'I just do the things I'm interested in,' said Anne. 'I come across things by accident, and if they look like they'll be fun, I grab the opportunity.

'I started editing by accident. About 13 years ago I bought the first edition of a beautiful magazine about the Wilsons Promontory area. But I noticed some errors, so I offered to edit the next edition. I've been *Coast* magazine's sub-editor ever since, and I've gradually taken on other editing clients, mostly in memoir and tourism.'

Anne's art gallery also came about through accidental opportunism. In 2013, Anne enrolled in a course in African mud-cloth – a technique using natural earth pigments to dye fabric. She enjoyed it enough to start applying earth pigments to canvas instead of fabric.

'I started to source pigments locally,' said Anne. 'Most of the pigments I use come from our property on Corner Inlet.

'With a lot of encouragement from a local artist, I held an exhibition and sold some work. Then other local artists started to use the natural earth pigments, so I decided we needed a place to exhibit. I opened a little gallery to display our work, and it's really taken off.'

When the building across the road from the gallery came on the market, Anne jumped at the chance to turn it into a cafe.

'I could see the need for an artistic little cafe in Foster,' said Anne. 'People would come into the gallery on weekends and ask, "where's the best place to go for coffee?" And we'd have to send them away.

'So I decided to create the gallery and cafe as sister businesses. The décor in the two buildings is the same, with earth pigments the major focus. We cross-promote between them.'

With French exams, editing, art, the gallery, and the cafe, you'd think that Anne has a busy enough retirement. But she's not easily satisfied. Recently she bought an abandoned bakery in a nearby town, and she dreams of getting it up and running.

'It's a gorgeous, century-old building with a magnificent Scotch [woodfired bakers'] oven,' said Anne. 'I'm hoping it will supply the cafe and the wider local area.'

Grabbing opportunities without making plans

Anne has never been keen on planning. She's a person who likes to take advantage of opportunities as they come along, without worrying too much about the end goal.

She spent no time planning her cafe's growth, thinking about its turnover, or setting targets for the number of cups of coffee to sell each day.

When Anne first thought about opening a cafe, she planned to secure a bank loan to buy the building. But the bank wanted a detailed business plan and financial forecast, and Anne wasn't interested.

'I started to write the business plan the bank wanted, and my heart just sank,' said Anne. 'They wanted me to make predictions and decisions for things I had no idea about – like how much the cafe would turn over and what our profit forecasts were.

'I decided right then to find a different way to make it work. I didn't want to make some kind of wild guess that I didn't have any confidence in. I was lucky enough to be able to take a lump sum from my superannuation. I was able to buy the building without getting a bank loan.

'I know many business owners and advisors would disagree, but so far my inclination has worked. I find excellent advice, tradespeople, and staff. I try to create a positive team atmosphere and lead by example – working hard, treating people respectfully, and making sure we all enjoy ourselves.

'I like to wait for opportunities to emerge, evaluate them, then trust my intuition, grab the great ones, get the right people involved, and work hard.'

Getting help when it's needed

Anne might not be a planner, but she understands the value of seeking good advice. 'I didn't know the first thing about starting a cafe,' said Anne. 'I knew that I'd need good advice if I was going to make this work. I was really blessed to find exactly the support I needed.'

Chapter 6: The accidental cafe

Anne contacted her friends Daniel and Hilary, who own Prom Coast Ice Cream, to ask about selling their ice-cream in her cafe. They quickly became her business advisors. Daniel and Hilary had moved to Gippsland to run the beach kiosk at Walkerville and establish Prom Coast Ice Cream.

'Daniel and Hilary knew everything I could possibly need to know about starting a food business,' said Anne. 'They held my hand every step of the way. During the setup I consulted them on every issue.

'I didn't know anything about making coffee, so I relied on Daniel for advice. He's a coffee aficionado, so exactly the right person to ask.

'He found a second-hand coffee machine that was perfect for us. He chose the grinder. He made me realise that the grinder is just as important as the espresso machine. And he made me realise that using high-quality milk is a must.

'I wanted to have excellent coffee, and Daniel guided me in the right direction. We're using a local roaster, who creates a blend just for us. We get so many comments about the quality of our coffee. It's really helping us to build a reputation.

'I had no idea what was needed, but Daniel and Hilary helped me to plan everything. They understood the health regulations. They knew exactly what equipment we would need and how to design a workable menu. They even helped me find the right staff.

'I don't think I could possibly have succeeded without their help.'

With trusted advisors on her side, Anne quickly learned to be selective in listening to other people's suggestions.

'In the early days, I had a lot of people coming in and telling me what I should be doing,' said Anne. 'Everyone had an opinion about what hours we should be open or what we should be selling.

'I learned to let people tell me anything they wanted. I listened, but I didn't do anything without asking Daniel and Hilary for their opinion. As time went by I realised I needed to regard them as consultants, and pay them for their services. That made me feel more comfortable about my constant phone calls, emails, and texts!

'I'd suggest that anyone who is thinking of starting a cafe needs trusted advisors who really understand the business.'

What's in a name?

Cow Cow might seem like an unusual name for a cafe. But for Anne, it's a perfect fit.

'This is dairy and beef-farming country,' said Anne. 'My husband and I own a cattle property and many of my earth-pigment paintings are inspired by cows.

'The name just seemed to fit. When I took over the building in May 2018, I painted a big cow with the words "Cow Cow" on it, and hung it in the window.

'I put a sign in the window saying the cafe would open in September. It took us a few months longer than expected, but the sign helped generate interest.

'We've got a modern, minimalist aesthetic. The cafe is open plan, with the kitchen visible to everyone in the cafe. The walls are grey and white, and all the paintings are black and white earth pigments. I think it's welcoming and fresh.'

Covering costs

Cow Cow opened in December 2018, just ahead of the region's peak summer tourist season. After six months of operation, it was just about busy enough to cover its costs. While establishing the cafe is taking longer than Anne expected, she's feeling comfortable with its progress.

'I've always said the cafe has to pay its own way,' said Anne. 'I don't expect to make a living from it, and I don't need it to make a big profit, but I do need to make sure I'm not losing money.'

Anne employs a bookkeeper who keeps track of her various businesses.

Chapter 6: The accidental cafe

'I'm not a numbers person,' said Anne. 'But I do understand how important it is to keep track of the figures, wages, taxes, and so on.

'I remember being pretty shocked when I saw the cafe's first financial report, six weeks after we opened. I'd gone with the perceived wisdom of the region, that we'd make money in the January holiday season. But maybe that wasn't realistic for a brand new business.

'After six weeks of operating, we were $28,000 in the red, though there were a few capital costs in there that will be one-offs. We've slowly turned that around, and it's just about holding its own now.

'I often wonder what it would be like for a younger person going into a cafe. I worry that it would be virtually impossible to make a good living from it.

'Someone told me early on that you can't make money from running a cafe. You might make money when you sell, but not while you're actually running it. I don't know whether that's right, but I'm glad I don't have any expectation of making money.'

Anne is conscious that staffing is her biggest expense and biggest risk.

'I want to make sure we pay people properly,' said Anne. 'I don't begrudge staff their full wages. They work hard and they deserve to be paid. But sometimes it's difficult to bring in enough income to cover the wages, especially when you're committed to really high-quality food.

'I was astonished to discover that most hospitality workers don't seem to get paid properly. My bookkeeper has put together a set of forms for people who start work with us. The staff always seem so surprised to get it. Invariably they've been paid cash before, without paying tax or getting superannuation.'

Staffing the cafe and gallery

Unlike many small-business owners, Anne hasn't experienced great difficulties with staffing. For her, it's not finding and retaining staff that cause problems: she's proud to claim she's got sensational staff. But paying staff and getting the roster right create ongoing challenges.

Cow Cow is a small cafe, with seating for just 20 people. Most of the time, it's a one- or two-person operation. The challenge for Anne is having back-up staff available when needed. She employs casual staff for weekends and holidays, and has a hospitality student on site one day a week.

'I didn't plan to be constantly in the cafe myself,' said Anne. 'I thought I'd have the place fully staffed, and I'd spend most of my time in the gallery.

'But so far it hasn't worked out like that. I need to be in the cafe every weekend, because of the crippling penalty rates.'

Even though Anne is much more hands-on in the cafe than she expected, she has no complaints.

'I enjoy being in the cafe so much. I really enjoy people. It's just really good fun.'

Not an owner-operator

Anne might own Cow Cow, but she's not the classic owner-operator of a small cafe. She can't operate the cafe alone, and that doesn't concern her.

'I'm never in the cafe by myself,' said Anne. 'I couldn't possibly do it all by myself. I didn't ever expect to work in the cafe every day, and I'm comfortable that I can't do everything myself.

'My husband keeps telling me that I should learn to make coffee, but I'm not confident I'd do a good job.'

Anne employs a full-time manager/barista, who makes most of the day-to-day decisions about operating the cafe.

'Sharni is the perfect person for the cafe,' said Anne. 'She's brilliant at what she does, and she can run the place completely by herself. She's also fully focused on making Cow Cow successful. She's a treasure beyond compare.

'I realise that I'm fully dependent on Sharni, and it will be a problem for me if she ever gets sick. But I'm conscious she needs to take holidays and have occasional days off.

'We have a hospitality student here once a week, and she's working out wonderfully. Sharni is starting to build her skills, so she'll be ready to take over when Sharni wants to travel.'

Beautiful food, great coffee

Anne is committed to ensuring Cow Cow sells top-quality food and coffee in a friendly and welcoming environment.

'People who come here often describe Cow Cow as a Melbourne-style cafe,' said Anne. 'I take it as a great compliment.

'Because of my love of all things French, we naturally seemed to gravitate towards French-style menu items. We've specialised in croissants. We also serve simple things like pies, pasties, sausage rolls, and sourdough rolls.

'Just before Cow Cow opened, a French pastry chef moved into town with her husband and two children. Her timing was perfect. She does most of our cooking, and I'm hoping that she'll take over the new bakery.

'Presentation of the food is really important to me. Our crockery, glassware, and cutlery are quirky, and we plate the food very carefully.

'So often when we take a meal out, people comment about how beautiful it looks. I like every plate to be like a little work of art.

'I think it's my job to create an atmosphere that makes people feel happy and welcome. And I absolutely love that side of it.'

An adventure, not a job

For Anne, the cafe and its sister gallery are an adventure, rather than a job.

'Even though I've not made much money from either venture, I wouldn't change the experience for anything.'

NEWBIES IN THE CAFE

Anne hasn't lost sight of her original plan: to set the cafe up and then leave it in the hands of her manager.

'I'm developing the business with Sharni, and I'd love her to take it over one day, though of course only time will tell. Owning the building is a big plus: in the short term I don't have the burden of paying rent, and in the long-term I hope to earn an income by leasing the business.'

'The cafe is a big commitment. It's seriously dented my bank balance. But it's such good fun, and while I'm enjoying it and it's roughly paying for itself, I'll keep at it.'

Chapter 7

It's not work when you love the industry

Newbie: Anthea Williams

Cafe: Keswick Cafe, Keswick Barracks SA (2018 –)

Previous occupation: University manager

NEWBIES IN THE CAFE

In 2012, Anthea Williams faced a choice: take an extended holiday in Italy and see the Monaco Grand Prix or buy a run-down cafe in the Adelaide suburb of Forestville.

Was it really a choice? Of course she bought the cafe! Anthea's journey into hospitality began.

Today, Anthea owns and operates the successful Keswick Cafe within Adelaide's Keswick Barracks, part of the Australian Defence Force. She sells more than 25 kilograms of coffee every week. She's passionate about the cafe industry and couldn't be happier. But achieving success took some time.

From university administration to cafe owner

Anthea left senior university management to launch her new life as a cafe owner. She said goodbye to a job that had her managing 75 academic staff in health sciences at an Adelaide university to become her own boss in a tiny cafe that, when she bought it, was selling roughly one kilogram of coffee per week.

'I suddenly realised I'd lost my passion for university work,' said Anthea. 'I had always loved my job. I was well paid and very busy, but suddenly it just didn't seem to be enough. It was time for a change.'

When the university restructured, Anthea grabbed the opportunity to accept early retirement and look for something new. Within a few months, her husband also took early retirement from his engineering job. They decided to become small-business owners together.

'My closest friends thought I was mad when I left the university,' said Anthea. 'It's hard to get a high-level position in university management, and I was walking away from a secure job.'

Initial research as cafe customers

Anthea didn't leave her university job with a burning desire to open a cafe. But once she decided to start a small business, the dream of cafe ownership took hold.

Chapter 7: It's not work when you love the industry

'I've always wanted to own my own business,' said Anthea. 'I love food and I love catering for events. I love working with people. I'm a real coffee snob. Most days I drink about 20 shots of coffee. A cafe seemed like a logical choice.

'We spent months doing market research, visiting many, many cafes while we decided what to do. We probably visited 100 cafes, many of which were on the market. We spent hours observing staff and customers, and monitoring how each place operated.

'I realised later that our research taught us a lot about customer interaction, but we didn't learn much about how a cafe runs. We had no real understanding of the work involved, and we particularly didn't understand the long hours. We didn't realise there was so much cleaning!

'Just as we were making plans for an extended holiday to Italy, we found Cafe Leader. It ticked a lot of boxes for us. It was run down and in desperate need of a makeover. It was close to our home. And it looked like a place that we could put our stamp on and make our own.

'The trip to Italy was postponed indefinitely, and we set about learning how to operate a cafe.'

A terrifying start

Anthea and her husband had no experience in the cafe industry and little understanding of what the work would be like.

'We both did a two-day coffee course and I did my mandatory training in food safety and work health and safety,' said Anthea. 'We had a one-week handover with the previous owners, and then we were on our own.

'Those first weeks and months were absolutely terrifying. I can remember wondering what we'd done. The first time I had to cook an order for eggs benedict, I dropped the eggs because my hands were shaking so much!

'At first I was totally out of my depth. I wasn't confident about what I was doing, and I had so much to learn about how to run the business.

'But it didn't take too long for my confidence to grow. I realised that customers can't see what you're going through, and they're also not particularly interested. They interact with you when they first arrive, then they switch off until their order arrives. If everything looks good, they don't think about what you've gone through to produce it. People eat with their eyes.

'I also realised early on that the quality of ingredients makes all the difference. Right from the beginning I was determined to have top-quality food. That means it was always good to eat, even if my presentation wasn't spot on at first.'

Buying a run-down business

When Anthea and her husband bought Cafe Leader, it was run down and doing very little trade. But they could see its potential: it was next door to a big music store, close to the army barracks, and near The Adelaide Showground.

'As soon as we put an "under new management" sign in the window, our trade started to pick up,' said Anthea. 'We started to grow quite quickly, and our confidence grew with it.'

Anthea believes that buying an existing business – even a business that is badly run down – is easier than starting from scratch, particularly for people who are new to the industry.

'If I'd tried to start from nothing and fit out a new cafe, I would have been totally lost,' she said. 'I would have had no idea what to buy and how to set it up.

'I was able to learn the business slowly, and gradually change the format to suit our needs and those of our customers. I needed to work in it for a while and get an idea of what I was doing before I could make any decisions about equipment and fitout.

'We gradually turned Cafe Leader into a wonderful environment. Because we were next door to a music store, we put in a piano, ukulele, and guitar. We had lots of musicians coming through, and they'd have spontaneous jamming sessions. It created a fabulous atmosphere.'

Willing to ask questions

Anthea was conscious that she started out with little understanding of the hospitality industry. Her solution was to ask questions, listen to suggestions, and not take feedback too personally.

'In the early days I was like a sponge, soaking up all the information I could,' said Anthea.

'I actively sought feedback from customers. I'd ask whether they enjoyed their coffee and whether they thought the food should be done differently. I monitored what was popular and what didn't get eaten.

'I also spent a lot of time asking questions of suppliers. Every time I wasn't sure about something, I asked someone who was likely to know more than me. I remember asking all sorts of questions about which eggs would poach best. And we tried 13 different types of bacon before eventually deciding which one to use.

'I was up front with suppliers. I was willing to tell them I was new to the business and was looking for their suggestions. I listened to their ideas, but I always made my own decisions.

'I've always felt very comfortable asking questions. I don't worry that I'll come across as an idiot. I think my experience of managing staff makes me confident enough to ask.'

It takes time to make a living

Even though Cafe Leader flourished from the beginning, it took some time for Anthea and her husband to make a living.

'We thought we would make money quickly,' said Anthea. 'We had about $50,000 in reserve, and we thought that was plenty to see us through.

'But that money went quickly. There were so many expenses we didn't think about. Even though the cafe was growing, it took a long time to become profitable.'

Anthea isn't convinced that her research and planning were helpful in getting the business established.

'We did a lot of planning before we opened,' she said. 'We had all the plans in the world, but the money side of the business wasn't anything like we expected. The money just disappeared! It was well over 12 months before we started to make any income.'

'We wrote a business plan because everyone said we needed one. But we didn't stick to it, and I don't think it helped us at all. What we wrote in the business plan didn't apply to the reality we were living.

'I wish we'd had a better understanding of the financial side of owning a cafe before we bought Cafe Leader. We needed to be more realistic about the business and how time-consuming the paperwork is.

'The business management is so critical. And it's much more complex than the food and coffee. Our first year would have been less stressful if we'd understood it more.'

Business partner and life partner

Anthea and her husband bought Cafe Leader together and expected to both work in the business.

'We thought it would be fun to work together,' said Anthea. 'In our business plan we agreed that I'd focus on operating the cafe, and my husband would look after the business management. But we didn't really stick to our plans. We ended up both trying to do the same things.

'Looking back, I think that going into business together was one of the poorer choices we've made. It wasn't easy.

'I don't honestly think that couples should work together. The business is all-consuming, and there's nothing else to talk about at the end of the day.

'We worked together for two years, and most days I fired him. Eventually he realised I meant it, and he went back to engineering.'

A sudden end

About three years after Anthea took over Cafe Leader, its lease was due for renewal. The cafe was flourishing. Anthea had established her dream business and was making a reasonable income. But overnight, everything changed.

'The landlord announced that he'd like us to vacate, just like that,' said Anthea. 'He wouldn't renew the lease. He didn't want to buy the business from me. And he didn't want me to sell it. He simply wanted vacant possession.

'I was absolutely mortified. I'd built the business and it was a flourishing cafe. And within a few weeks, I was closed. It was like the end of the world for me.'

Anthea turned to her friends and customers for support while she decided what to do.

'I had a coffee with a customer who had become a good friend. I remember bursting into tears. My world was coming to an end and I was losing my business.

'He reassured me the best he could. He was full of the typical rhetoric: "One door closes but another opens" – that kind of thing.

'But this man is an enabler. He's a soldier based at Keswick, and he's good at making things happen.

'Before long he suggested that I should try opening a cafe within the barracks. It was a radical suggestion, but it sounded like a fabulous idea.'

A civilian inside the military

To say that Anthea took on a challenge is an understatement: civilians don't typically open businesses within military bases. But the seed was sown, and Anthea was committed.

'It took six months of hard work from when we first had the idea to when we finally opened,' said Anthea.

'The benefit of the idea was clear. Keswick Barracks had no place where personnel could meet each other for coffee. There was no decent coffee on site. Cafe Leader had been their meeting place, but it was closed.

'Achieving the approvals to put a cafe on the barracks was a big undertaking. It went to public tender, and we needed statements of support. But the approvals happened eventually.'

Anthea was given two heritage-listed junk rooms as the site for her new cafe. The rooms were full of rubbish and hadn't been used for years. The heritage listing ensured there were tight conditions with the fitout.

'At times it felt as though I had endless brick walls in front of me,' said Anthea. 'I felt like little David negotiating with Goliath.

'I needed an engineer to handle the design within the constraints of heritage listing. I needed a lawyer for the contractual side.

'But my passion for the business kept me going. Thankfully I had enough cafe experience to be confident about what I was doing. It was all well worth it.'

Keswick Cafe opened in April 2018, about six months after Cafe Leader closed. It quickly became everything that Anthea hoped it would be.

Being a cafe employee

In the months between closing Cafe Leader and opening Keswick Cafe, Anthea worked as a cook in someone else's cafe.

'It was great for me to work in another kitchen,' said Anthea. 'I learned a lot from that experience. I wish I'd done it before we bought Cafe Leader, because I would have gone in with a much better understanding of the business.

'I turned out some beautiful meals at that cafe. We were doing up to 150 plates per service, and the pace nearly killed me. But it was a fantastic learning experience. I learned a lot more about working at speed and about food presentation. I also learned about what it's like to be an employee.

'Seeing the back operation of someone else's cafe made me more conscious about cleanliness and food safety. It also increased my commitment to treating my staff well.'

Doing every job in the cafe

Anthea has a hands-on approach to managing her business. There's no job in the cafe that she won't do, and no job she'd ask a team member to do that she won't do herself.

'I believe you've got to know your business every way possible,' said Anthea. 'You've got to know it backwards, inside out, and upside down.

'I also believe that cafe owners should be able to do every job in the business. If I couldn't, what would I do if someone was away?

'I'm convinced that a successful cafe needs the owner to be present. I don't need to be at the cafe every minute it's open, but I need to be very hands-on. I'm in there doing everything alongside the team. It's my responsibility to build up the clientele and create the business I want it to be.

'I'm in the cafe every day. Most days, I do the opening by myself because it doesn't make sense to pay staff when it's quiet. Then I leave after the lunch rush, and let the team close up. I have my afternoons to myself, which gives me a good balance.'

NEWBIES IN THE CAFE

Creating the right environment

Anthea believes that creating the right environment for the team helps to create the right environment for customers.

'I try really hard to create an environment that people love to work in,' said Anthea. 'I want my team to love what they do. They need to enjoy their work. It sounds like a cliché, but it's true: a happy team leads to happy customers.

'My approach to staffing is to recruit slowly and fire quickly. I employ people largely because they'll fit the team, not because they've got all the skills we need. I can teach the skills.

'I have a fabulous team, including a manager who treats the business like it's her own. They create the environment that makes people feel welcome.'

More than food and coffee

Anthea thinks that successful cafes are about more than good food and great coffee.

'Food and coffee are obviously important,' said Anthea. 'But they're not enough. The cafe needs to be a place where people want to be.

'We've created a warm, friendly, welcoming environment for the personnel who work at Keswick. We've got comfy couches and carpet on the floor. We play quiet music and get in good quality newspapers and magazines. We've created a place where people can have some time out.

'This is a tri-service site, with personnel from the navy, army, and air force working side-by-side. I often hear people say they meet new people at the cafe, even though they've worked on site for years.'

Living the dream

Anthea is firmly committed to the cafe life and has no plans of returning to a 9-to-5 job. But she's also conscious that it's not a job she could do forever.

Chapter 7: It's not work when you love the industry

'I live and breathe the cafe,' said Anthea. 'It's my whole life, and I love it. For me it's not work. I'm absolutely passionate about the industry.

'But I'm physically tired. The long hours wear thin after a while. I'll go on for as long as I can, because I love it.'

Anthea suggests that people need to think very carefully before taking on a cafe. It might not be what they expect.

'My advice to anyone thinking about starting a cafe is that it's incredibly rewarding, but the rewards may not be financial. It's about working with people and having a passion for food and coffee. It's very hard work and very long hours.

'It takes a long time to see any financial reward. It's possible that the financial reward won't happen until you sell.

'I'm not in it for the financial gain, though I'm pleased to say that does come eventually. The hours are unpredictable and it dominates your whole life. You have to be passionate about it or you wouldn't be able to do it.

'But I get so much from the business. I love every aspect of it.'

Chapter 8

From nothing to success and back again

Newbie: Aimee*

Cafe: Cafe & roastery in regional Australia (2003 – 2017)

Previous occupation: Hydrogeologist

*Name changed to preserve anonymity

Chapter 8: From nothing to success and back again

In 2002, Aimee was a government-employed hydrogeologist. A career in science stretched ahead.

Then her life took a left turn. She married and, with her new husband, embarked on an adventure in coffee. Together they established a busy cafe and roastery in regional Australia. The adventure lasted until 2017, when Aimee decided to sell.

In the 15 years she operated the cafe and roastery, Aimee navigated a full business cycle. She started with nothing, developed a highly successful business, considered national expansion, and stayed past the time when it would have been wise to sell.

As the business grew, Aimee's health suffered, the business contracted, and problems appeared. She closed the cafe side of the business, liquidated the roastery, re-opened as a smaller operation, and eventually decided to sell. She's now working outside the coffee industry.

A year of research

Before opening the cafe, Aimee devoted a full year to planning and research.

'My husband persuaded me that we should go into coffee,' said Aimee. 'He thought we'd make a lot of money, and we had very big dreams.

'I knew I had a lot to learn and I wanted to make sure we did everything properly. So I made business planning my full-time job for a year. I taught myself how to roast, I planned every aspect of the roastery and cafe, and my husband and I looked for a place to set up shop.

'I knew our product had to be spot on. A few months before we opened I bought a commercial espresso machine and set it up at home. I practised making coffee until I was completely confident that I had everything right. On the day we opened the doors, I knew exactly what I was doing, and I was confident our coffee was top quality.

'We established our business in a regional centre that offered everything we needed. It's a tourist destination, has a strong artisan community, and is a good place to raise a family. It seemed like a great alternative to a capital city.

'The location worked for us, and the cafe was a hit with the community from the day we opened. People would drive for miles to visit us. One fellow stopped on a trip with his friends, and the following week he brought his wife on a six-hour round trip for a cup of coffee!'

Setting up for growth

Aimee and her husband established their business with growth in mind.

'Our idea was to sell coffee online,' said Aimee. 'Online shopping was just starting to take off and our vision was very clear: we wanted to sell top-quality beans for the home market.

'Our location really helped. Visitors to the region could try our coffee, then order online for home delivery.

'Our original idea included having cafes around the country. We trademarked everything and set up our business systems with growth in mind. We were ready to take on the world!

'In 2005, about three years after we opened, we installed a sophisticated point-of-sale system that could support up to 900 stores and multiple currencies. We had a bump screen for the coffee* – probably the first bump screen in our region. And we had buzzers so that customers could go to the park and nearby shops while they were waiting for their order.'

A detailed plan for business setup

Aimee and her husband rented an empty shop in a new industrial estate. Within one month of signing the lease, they opened the doors. Aimee credits her detailed business plan with their speedy start.

A bump screen automatically displays orders sent by the point-of-sale, with the orders 'bumped off' as they're made.

'We had the roastery and a tiny cafe in the same shop,' said Aimee. 'Because I'd done so much planning and I already owned the equipment, we were able to open the doors very quickly. I had a fantastic set-up plan.

'Right from the beginning, I had a vision in my head of what the business would be like. But I only ever wrote down the set-up plan. I didn't record the long-term vision, and I now realise that I didn't think it through carefully enough.

'I wish I'd written down my vision and put it in a place where I could see it every day. That would have reminded me what I was doing and why.'

Instead of following the vision, Aimee and her husband got caught up in growing and running the cafe.

'We got so caught up in how busy we were that we lost sight of what we wanted to achieve,' said Aimee.

'We listened to customers and let the cafe grow rapidly, when our real interest was roasting the beans. We ended up with a successful business that wasn't balanced the right way for us.'

'Most of the time we operated the business, I didn't have a good sense of our direction. I didn't ever write an operating plan and an expansion plan, so I didn't have anything to work towards.

'I also didn't write an exit plan. I now believe that every business owner should write their exit plan before they open the doors. We should have known before we started when we thought we'd sell the business and what we'd do if things weren't going well.'

A simple cafe, with a focus on the coffee

For Aimee, the business was always about the coffee, not the food.

'It was roasting that I was passionate about,' said Aimee. 'The cafe was always intended to be secondary.

'I knew I didn't want to cook food on site, so we only sold food that could be brought in pre-made. At first, we only sold a few cakes and slices. As we grew, we let the menu become more complex and started to sell full meals.

'The cafe gradually took over, because it was popular. We listened to what customers wanted, and let that set our direction.'

When they opened, the cafe was very small, with just 18 seats. 'I remember getting advice from a designer when we were choosing the furniture for the cafe,' said Aimee. 'He asked whether we wanted people to linger in the cafe, or whether we wanted them to have their coffee and move on.

'Of course with just 18 seats, we wanted people to move on. We needed to have new people on those seats every hour or so. So with his advice we chose stools instead of comfy chairs. We wanted it to look good, without being too comfortable.'

Slow growth, then a boom

As with many small businesses, the cafe–roastery grew more slowly in the early months than Aimee and her husband had hoped.

'For the first few months, our growth was quite slow,' said Aimee. 'Initially it was just the two of us working there, and we were open six days a week. Because our expenses were low, we broke even quickly, but we didn't turn over a lot of money at first and it was a long time before we earned much.

'It was a massive pressure on us both, going into the business together and not having any guaranteed income. But we didn't really need to earn much because we were so busy with the business. It was all-consuming.

'We employed our first staff member about six months after we opened. But I wasn't ready. I hadn't thought through how we'd manage staff and how we'd explain our vision to them. I also didn't explain their boundaries properly – like what things they could make decisions about and when they needed to talk to me.

'I think business owners should write a staff manual. But it's something I didn't get around to doing myself.

Chapter 8: From nothing to success and back again

'Once we started to employ staff, we grew quickly – probably too quickly, when I look back on it. There was no time to reflect on what we were doing, because there was always so much to do.

'We expanded the cafe three times over the years, and moved the roastery to another site. Eventually the cafe could sit 110 people. It became a big operation, and keeping track of both the cafe and the roastery was very difficult.

'When the cafe was big and successful, we started to achieve real financial success. I remember one month we made $30,000 profit. But it came at a cost and my health started to suffer.

'Like so many small-business owners, I was working in the business every minute of the day, and I never had any time to work on the business. It was so difficult to take a breath and reflect on what was happening. The pace was manic.

'I ended up with a very successful business, but it wasn't the business I wanted. My heart wasn't in the cafe side of the business, and I found it was increasingly stressful.

'When the business was at its peak, I thought a lot about expanding. But by then I was getting tired. And I had the children to think about. I didn't want to be too busy because I wanted to be part of their childhoods.

'I was also conscious that expanding would have given us a very different type of business. I would have moved away from the day-to-day work and employed all sorts of advisors. It would have taken me completely away from roasting, which was what I enjoyed.'

Juggling family and business

Aimee and her husband were newly married when they opened their cafe–roastery.

'We were both captured by the dream of roasting fresh beans for the domestic market,' said Aimee. 'At the time it sounded more appealing to me than working as a scientist. My mother had owned a restaurant, so I had a reasonable idea of what we were taking on.'

Not long after they opened the business, the first of their two children was born. 'Looking back, I wish I'd taken time off to be with the kids, and left my husband to run the business. But I didn't do that. I went back to work when both the children were very young. I took them to work with me and they grew up in and around the cafe.'

After a few years of running the business together, Aimee and her husband decided that it might be easier if they worked separately.

'It was a very difficult time,' said Aimee. 'We had different ideas about what should be done in the business, and it started to affect our marriage. We had a lot of pressure from our families.

'It got to the stage where we had to decide whether we preferred the marriage or the business. We chose the marriage, and my husband found another job. That saved our marriage, but it meant I took on full responsibility for the business. His job involved travelling, so a lot of the time it was just me with the growing business and two children.'

Taking a wage from the business

Right from the day the cafe–roastery opened, Aimee was determined she wouldn't join the ranks of small-business owners who only take an income if there's money left over after the bills have been paid.

'As soon as the business was operating successfully, my husband and I set ourselves up as employees and took an income,' said Aimee. 'We paid ourselves a proper wage. I was an employee, just like our other employees.

'As it turned out, that was my saviour. As a wage earner, I was covered by WorkCover. When I injured myself at work, I was covered and that meant I could keep the business operating. It gave me time to make decisions. If I hadn't had WorkCover, I probably would have had to simply close straight away.'

Chapter 8: From nothing to success and back again

Building customer loyalty

In the early days, Aimee had a traditional coffee loyalty card. Customers had a card that was clipped each time they purchased a coffee, and every tenth coffee was free.

'It was a reasonable way to build loyalty, but I started to get really annoyed with our system,' said Aimee. 'People always wanted a more valuable coffee when it was free. So if they normally bought cup size, they'd expect a jumbo size for the free one. And the loyalty card wasn't designed to help us stop that.'

When Aimee installed the point-of-sale system in 2005, she changed to a computer-based points system. Customers earned points for every purchase, and used their points towards free coffee or food.

'The automated system was much better,' said Aimee. 'It was fair, and it meant that people got loyalty points for everything they bought, not just for their coffee.'

Because the cafe was in a tourist region, Aimee used the loyalty program to attract tour buses into the cafe. 'Getting tourist buses to stop was a big deal for us. We wanted them to try our coffee, then order online once they got home.

'At first I gave a free coffee to bus drivers if they stopped at the cafe. But I soon realised that some drivers would get their free coffee from us, then send their passengers somewhere else to give the driver a quiet break.

'So I applied the same loyalty system to bus drivers. The drivers earned points when their passengers spent money with us. Some drivers got a free meal every week because they brought in so many customers. It worked really well for us.'

The beginning of the end

Even though the cafe–roastery was a big success, it took its toll on Aimee.

'It got to the point where I was so exhausted I couldn't think straight,' said Aimee. 'I started to make poor decisions and became very unwell.

'It was relentless. We were open six days a week and were busy all the time. There was never a break. In theory I could operate the business from home through the point-of-sale system, but it just didn't seem to be working.

'Having the business in two different locations didn't help, particularly as I wanted to be roasting coffee, not operating a super-busy cafe.

'I didn't realise it at the time, but one of the staff had started taking money from us. It ended up being quite a lot of money. All of a sudden, the cafe wasn't doing as well as it had been. We were still as busy as ever, but financially we were going backwards.

'It reached a crisis point when I was being choked to death by the business and became really unwell. I wished that I didn't have it any more, but I couldn't see how to get out. The problem with a business like a cafe is that you can't just decide to sell it one day. You have to prepare to sell it. It takes ages.'

The decision to close

In 2010, Aimee put the cafe side of the business on the market.

'I tried to sell the cafe through an agent, but no one was interested. On paper the cafe didn't look successful, even though we were busy.

'Eventually I was so tired of it that I closed the cafe and sold the equipment to someone who was willing to take over the lease. They started a new cafe on the site.

'Even though that decision cost me money, it meant that I was free of the cafe and could focus my attention on the roastery. It gave me time to recover my health.'

Saying goodbye to the roastery

Aimee continued to own the roastery for some few years after she sold the main cafe. Her health improved and she was back doing the work she loved. But a simple injury brought it all to a halt.

'I'd been closed for a short holiday,' said Aimee. 'And the day I returned to start roasting, about a week before I planned to re-open, I injured both thumbs picking up a sack of beans. Working was impossible. I needed surgery and several weeks to recover.

'I saw it as a sign: it was time for me to get out. I put the roastery on the market and it sold quite quickly. Selling it was such a relief.'

Would she do it again?

Aimee has no regrets about her 15 years in the coffee industry, but she doesn't have any plans to return. She also thinks that staying in hydrogeology would have given her a more stable income.

'I work in sales now, so I still deal with people every day, but it's different. I work for someone else, and that makes a nice change.

'I think customer-service businesses are difficult. So many customers expect to get something for nothing. It's almost as though they don't understand the costs involved in producing their food and coffee, and they forget that someone has to pay for everything.

'My advice to anyone considering a cafe business is to plan ahead, keep your eye on your staff, and don't trust anyone.

'I also think people need to remember that it's just a business. Your business is not your life. It's easy to let it consume everything, but it shouldn't.

'People who own small businesses should only make decisions that are good choices for them. I let myself be swayed by what other people wanted. And business owners need to keep their finger on the pulse always. They need to understand everything that's happening. I took my eyes off the business because I was stressed and unwell, and that's when things started to go wrong.

NEWBIES IN THE CAFE

'I think that anyone starting a cafe needs a good operating plan and an exit plan. It makes sense to review the business every three years or so and decide whether they want to continue.

'Looking back, I think my biggest problem was that I didn't pay enough attention to myself. I've always been able to handle stress well, and I like being busy. But I didn't make any time for myself at all and I didn't rest. I was ill and struggling with the business, and that's when I started to make bad decisions.

'I was too exhausted to leave. I wanted to get out, but I didn't know how to.'

Chapter 9

Start small + grow slow = a recipe for success

Newbie: Reg James

Cafe: Bay21, Forest Hill Vic (2018 –)

Previous occupation: Retail

NEWBIES IN THE CAFE

The day before Reg James opened his cafe in the Melbourne suburb of Forest Hill, he realised he was taking a risk.

Reg had left behind a secure job in retail management to open Bay21, a 'grab and go' cafe near a refurbished office building.

'The council came in and signed everything off the day before we opened,' said Reg. 'I just remember standing here after the inspectors left.

'I was on my own, and it suddenly dawned on me that I was about to do something new. Something that I had absolutely no real idea about. How was I going to do it?

'I went from being incredibly excited to wondering what I'd done!

'I put a lot of pressure on myself that day. I stood there thinking, *You've got to get this right Reg.* I was about to have people coming in for coffee, and I needed to get it right the first time. I figured there was no room for mistakes.'

Reg took his big risk in March 2018. Today, he's operating a small but successful cafe. And he's doing exactly what he wants to be doing.

A life-changing injury

It was a running injury that gave Reg the time and courage he needed to leave retail and move into hospitality. 'I'd had a long career in retail,' said Reg, 'and I was ready for a change. The running injury forced me to have time off work, and I started to think seriously about opening a cafe.

'I'd always wanted a cafe, and my wife and I had been talking about it for years. Our idea was that she'd do the cooking and I'd make the coffee.

'Being injured gave me the time I needed to research and plan. I decided to start small, because my wife wasn't ready to leave her job.

'I began to look at the opportunities available, and I thought seriously about a franchise. I was tempted to either buy into a cafe chain or a franchise coffee van with a designated area.

'I'd gathered all the information and was close to signing a contract when I stumbled across a cafe coach. It was the coach, Simon, who helped me figure out the best way to move forward.'

Working with a cafe coach

Reg met Simon O'Brien, an independent cafe coach who helps cafe newbies to get started in the industry.

'Simon helped me work out that franchising wasn't the best option for me,' said Reg. 'He was independent, and he helped me understand the costs involved in franchising. I hadn't really considered all the details. I'd definitely glossed over the fees, thinking they were standard.

'But Simon made me realise that I could start the same type of business under my own name, without paying for someone else's name to be above the door. In an independent cafe, I could do all the same things in the business, but be in complete control.'

Reg says that working with a cafe coach was the best decision he made.

'Before I met Simon, I was only getting information from people with a stake in the outcome,' said Reg. 'They wanted me to buy into their idea, so the information they gave me was narrow.

'But Simon knows the industry inside out. He asked endless questions and helped me work out what was best for me. His only interest was making my new business a success. I was able to use his knowledge to make the right decisions for me. And I didn't ever feel that he was sending me down a particular path because it was what he wanted.

'Because I hadn't worked in hospitality before, it was enormously useful to have someone to help me learn and guide me through the decisions.

'If I hadn't met Simon I'd probably be sitting in my coffee van right now, wondering how to get busier, how to meet the repayments, and how to make a living. Instead, I've got a solid little business.'

NEWBIES IN THE CAFE

A one-man operation

Reg operates Bay21 by himself. He might be his own boss, but he's also the barista, cashier, sandwich toaster, milkshake maker, bookkeeper, stock controller, website developer, and social media writer. And that's just the way he likes it.

'I always knew that I wanted to be very, very hands-on in the business,' said Reg. 'I suppose I'm what you'd call a control freak.

'This is a small business that can easily be run by one person. It's like a coffee cart, but a cart with four walls and a roof and a little bit of seating. Most of what we sell is pre-prepped and everything is sold in takeaway packaging.'

When Reg first opened, he employed an experienced barista for a few weeks.

'I was conscious that I needed to get the coffee right from day one,' said Reg. 'First impressions are everything, and I was worried that my barista skills weren't up to scratch. Even though I'd done coffee training, I didn't have any experience as a barista.

'Having an experienced barista by my side really helped in those early weeks. It meant I could make sure that every coffee going out the door was top quality.

'But once I was confident about the coffee I was making, I let the barista go. My current goal is to get busy enough to have a second barista during the morning rush.'

Quality matters in a competitive market

Reg's number one priority is making sure that his coffee is spot on, every time. He sells a local roast, which is popular with his customers.

'Melbourne is a cafe-oriented place, and I'm always conscious that the competition is fierce,' said Reg.

'Just about anywhere in Melbourne, you can walk 150 metres down the street and stumble into three cafes. So it's extremely important that every customer who comes in here leaves with a great coffee and a great experience.

Chapter 9: Small start + grow slow = a recipe for success

'Every coffee I put out has to be perfect. I'm always thinking: Is it good enough for me to drink? Because if it's not, I'm not selling it.

'We have two big assets: quality coffee and convenience. Most of the people who come in here are time poor. We offer quality products that are quick and easy for them to choose.'

Making a living

Within a few weeks of opening, Bay21 was busy enough to cover its costs and give Reg a small income.

'I kept the overheads as low as possible and made sure I'd be able to handle the expenses. The business pays its own bills and I'm not relying on my own money to subsidise it, which is great. I'm able to take a small income, and hopefully that will grow into a full income some time soon.

'My model involves very low overheads. I did a simple fitout, and will add to it when the money is available. My current goals are to buy a dishwasher and a bigger milk fridge.'

Initial planning

Reg put a lot of effort into planning the business, drawing on the expertise of his cafe coach.

'Simon crunched all the numbers with me and guided me through every stage of the planning process,' said Reg. 'He really helped me to understand the work involved in securing the lease and organising the fitout.'

Reg believes the planning has paid off, even though he's not yet meeting his initial expectations.

'I'm close to two refurbished office buildings, and I did the planning on the assumption that the buildings would be full,' said Reg.

'I'd hoped the offices would lease quickly, but it hasn't worked out that way. One building is full, but the other still has a lot of empty space. Bay21 is definitely growing, and every time an office leases things get a bit better. But the growth is much slower than I'd expected.

'Simon and I did the planning on the assumption that I'd sell about 25 kilograms of coffee a week, based on Simon's experience of the industry. I'm now doing between eight and ten kilos, which is a lot less than I'd expected.

'Sometimes I get frustrated by the slow growth, but when I look at it objectively I can see that things are going OK. We're going in the right direction, and that's what matters. My wife, who is more level-headed than me, tells me that I should be patient. It's still a new business!'

Slow, steady growth is sustainable

Reg is confident that slow, steady growth will pay off in the long-term.

'While I'd like the business to grow more quickly, I'm conscious that slow growth is best for the business,' he said. 'Slow growth means that I can keep the quality high all the time.

'It also means I can try new ideas one at a time, and change things if they don't work. Banana bread is an example of that. I tried it and it didn't sell, so I moved on to something else. Whole fruit is another example. I thought that would be popular, but I was wrong. I just ended up eating a lot of fruit!'

Reg is convinced that initial planning is helpful, but it's important to be flexible.

'The initial planning helped me to get started,' he said. 'But I've realised that nothing is set in stone. You've got to be ready to go with the ebb and flow of the business. It's great to have an idea, but I think you have to be ready to change it 150 times before it becomes a reality.

'Just because I might want to do something a particular way, that doesn't mean it's the best choice for the business. If it's not what the customers want, I have to change.'

Unwanted advice

One thing that Reg hadn't anticipated about owning a cafe was the unwanted advice he got from everyone he met.

'I've found that everyone who has ever had a business has an idea to share,' said Reg. 'Everyone wanted to tell me what would go wrong, and not all the stories were helpful.

'Even though I was used to people giving advice in retail, I wasn't prepared for the sheer volume of it. I tried to listen to everyone, and it got very cluttered in my mind.

'I quickly learned not to listen to most people. I didn't want to be rude, but I really didn't need to hear their stories. I chose a core group of people I felt happy to get advice from, and started to ignore everyone else. Having Simon as my coach helped me to focus only on the helpful advice.'

Keeping track of the numbers

Reg puts a lot of time into tracking the business, reflecting on the numbers, and making little changes.

'I have multiple spreadsheets and I update them every day,' said Reg. 'I know exactly where the business is at.

'If I see a change in customers' buying patterns, I can respond straight away. I keep track of how much I sell every day of each item I stock.

'I set myself daily targets, particularly for coffee sales. I'm never happy with the number of coffees I do in a day. Coffee is about 45 per cent of my turnover, and I'd like it to be higher.'

Into the future

Reg has been bitten by the cafe bug, and now he can't imagine doing anything else.

'I'm staying in hospitality now,' said Reg. 'Some mornings when I come around the corner and see my shop window, I'm blown away to think that the place is mine. I get excited for the day ahead. Working for someone else was never like that.

'Being my own boss is important to me. I love having the flexibility to run it my own way. But the disadvantage is that the buck stops with me. If I mess it up, then it's messed up and I have to figure out what to do. Oh, and there's no such thing as annual leave.

'I find that it's mentally refreshing to work for myself and make all the decisions. I like the way I've been able to learn the business without the complexities of employing staff.'

While Reg loves working for himself, he's conscious that he needs to make sure the cafe doesn't completely take over his life.

'This business could be all-consuming,' said Reg. 'It could swallow every minute of every day if I let that happen. There's always something to do.

'So my wife and I try to make some core time for ourselves. Sometimes I make myself sit back and think about different things. I need to have other things in my life, and I need to clear my head sometimes. Running is good for that. Having a cafe that's only open five days a week is also helpful.'

Reg has long-term plans for a bigger cafe. 'In the back of my mind, I know that my wife and I want to own a cafe together,' he said.

'This isn't the one, because we can't do cooking here. What I don't know yet is whether we'll keep this one and get a second, or sell this one.

'This business is looking very positive. There's every sign that Bay21 has the potential to be a nice little business. But it will always be little.'

Hard work, but worth it

Like everyone who operates a cafe, Reg recognises that it's hard work.

'There are definitely some days when I wonder whether I've made the right decision. It's hard work and my income is small. But most of the time I'm pretty happy.

Chapter 9: Small start + grow slow = a recipe for success

'I'm also a big believer in not getting too settled in a business. If I become too comfortable, I might stop trying to improve. It would be easy for the business to start going south without me noticing.

'I don't want to become complacent. But I'm definitely happy doing what I'm doing. For now, this is the right business for me.'

Chapter 10

But where are the customers?

Newbie: Neill Hooper

Cafe: Haven Espresso, Stafford Heights Qld (2014 –2016)

Previous occupation: Advertising & marketing executive

Neill Hooper is living proof that 20 years' experience in advertising and marketing can't guarantee you'll be able to promote an independent suburban cafe.

In 2014, Neill left a career in advertising to open Haven Espresso in the Brisbane suburb of Stafford Heights. He expected that owning a cafe would bring him an easier life. Instead, it brought him close to financial disaster.

Eighteen months after opening Haven Espresso, Neill sold the business and returned to advertising.

Captured by the dream

Like many cafe newbies, Neill was captured by the dream of owning a cafe.

'I was completely obsessed with the cafe dream,' said Neill. 'I thought it would be like heading towards retirement, especially after working in advertising.

'Advertising is incredibly stressful, and I thought the cafe would be easier. I thought I would slow down, drink coffee all day, talk to people, and have a lovely time.

'It wasn't like that at all. Instead it was long hours, huge amounts of stress, and absolutely no money.'

A trial run with beef jerky

Before opening Haven Espresso, Neill was co-owner of a beef jerky business. Neill coordinated its marketing, while continuing with his freelance advertising career.

'I started the jerky business with three friends, and we ran it together for six years,' said Neill. 'It did quite well. We had a cafe out the front, which always looked busy.

'At first, we had someone else running the cafe for us, but then the four of us took it over. From that experience, I learned what was involved in setting up a cafe and I was confident I could do it on my own.'

NEWBIES IN THE CAFE

Neill left the jerky business when he realised he wanted to do things differently. His friends bought him out, giving him enough money to start his own cafe.

'I left the beef jerky business thinking I knew how to run a cafe,' said Neill. 'I'd seen some things I wanted to do differently, and I decided this was my opportunity. I was going to operate a cafe the way I wanted, and I expected it to be a success.

'I clearly remember thinking that I knew how to do things right, because I'd seen things done wrong elsewhere. I thought I wouldn't make the same mistakes as other people.'

A location that 'ticked the boxes'

Neill looked around Brisbane's northside for the best location for his cafe. He chose a strip of shops in Stafford Heights, about 10 km from Brisbane's CBD.

'It seemed like a great location,' said Neill. 'It ticked all the boxes for me – the other shops in the strip were busy, the rent was reasonable, there was no cafe close by, it was close to schools, and it was only one street from the main road.

'There hadn't been a cafe on the street before and, looking back, I wonder whether that made it a poor choice. If I'd bought an existing cafe, I would have bought its client base. Instead, I started from scratch.

'When I first opened I thought I'd chosen a great location. The local people seemed really excited to have a cafe in the street. I had a lot of people coming to try it out, and at first it seemed really busy.

'Not long after I opened, a couple who lived in the street turned up with a cake they'd baked for me and the staff, to welcome us! It was a lovely way to begin.

'But after that initially flurry of interest, the numbers didn't hold. And I could never figure out why.'

Chapter 10: But where are the customers?

An art gallery–cafe

Neill's vision for Haven Espresso involved more than an independent suburban cafe. His plan combined the cafe with a small art gallery.

'I'd always wanted an arty cafe,' said Neill. 'I've held a few photography exhibitions myself, and I know how hard it is to find affordable gallery space.

'So when I fitted out the cafe, I painted the walls completely white, and made the whole place very plain and simple. I rented the wall space to a different artist each month.'

The art gallery side of the business was a great success, but the income it generated was never going to be enough to keep the cafe afloat.

'To start with, I charged $200 a month for the gallery space,' said Neill. 'I gradually increased the price, and my goal was to get to $500 a month. But even that wasn't enough income to make a big difference to the cafe.

'The art gallery idea was incredibly popular. It was booked out for months ahead. And because the artwork was constantly changing, it made the cafe a really interesting place to be.

'I decided right from the beginning that I'd accept anyone's work. It wasn't my place to judge the quality.

'If someone wanted to exhibit in the cafe and they were willing to pay for the space, I was happy to give them a go. I wanted the space to be open to everyone. We had all sorts of artwork. Some of it was really striking.'

Looking for ways to bring people in

Within a few months of opening, Neill realised the cafe wasn't as busy as he needed it to be, and he started to look at ways to bring people through the door.

'I was constantly looking for ways to make more money,' said Neill. 'I kept wondering how I could use the space to bring in a few more dollars.

'One thing I tried was life-drawing classes on Wednesday nights. They became popular. I kept them informal – just an opportunity for people to get together and have a go at life drawing. We'd chat, have a glass of wine and do some drawing together.

'Even though the life drawing was popular enough for me to break even every time, the classes weren't a big money earner. And they didn't seem to influence how busy we were at other times.'

Neill discovered that each new idea involved extra work for little income.

'The art gallery was a great idea, but it created a lot of work,' said Neill. 'On the day the artist was hanging their work, I'd have to be at the cafe very early. Then we'd usually have an opening on a Friday night, which involved a late night and catering.

'The extra things were all enjoyable, but I was already working such long hours. They just made the days longer. And they didn't seem to make a huge difference to the income.'

Why listen to caution?

Neill's pre-cafe planning was coloured by his dreams of owning his own cafe. Even though he heard tales of caution, he thought his cafe would be different.

'I remember my friends asking why I'd want to own a cafe,' said Neill. 'They said I didn't like people enough to run a cafe. Maybe they were right. I know I like to be in control, and I thought that having my own business would be the perfect way to do that.

'Before I opened I spent some time with a successful cafe owner, looking at his setup and getting advice. He encouraged me not to open. Even though I understood his caution, I was positive and passionate. I didn't intend to fail! I started with plans to be a massive success.

'I also visited a cafe expo and went to a talk about new cafes. The two speakers advised anyone who was new to the industry not to

Chapter 10: But where are the customers?

open a cafe. Everyone laughed. That's not what we were there to hear! But I think they were serious.

'My guess is their advice is based on their understanding of how hard it is and how many people are likely to fail. They've made a success of it themselves, but they know they're amongst the few. They also know that it takes a very long time to achieve success.

'Of course I didn't listen. I was convinced I'd be different. I wasn't planning to fail!'

A simple approach to planning

Neill planned his cafe before opening, but all his planning was inside his head, for his own benefit.

'I didn't do a written business plan at all,' said Neill. 'I'm arrogant enough to think that it wouldn't have helped.

'I knew what I needed to sell to break even, and I think I understood the business well enough. I didn't need to write it down to know it. I didn't need a loan, so I didn't need to write a plan for anyone else.

'In theory it sounds like selling coffee is an easy way to make money. If it costs 50 cents to make a coffee and you sell it for $4.50, it should be very easy to make money.

'But you need to sell hundreds of coffees to make it work. There are so many costs that go into keeping a cafe open.'

Not enough sales

Neill knew he needed to sell about 20 kilograms of coffee a week to break even. Most of the time he operated Haven Espresso, he sold roughly half that amount.

'I just didn't have enough people coming through the door to keep the cafe afloat,' said Neill. 'The problem was so simple: I didn't have enough customers.

'But I couldn't figure out a way to fix things. There were days that I'd drive home crying my eyes out, because I couldn't figure it out.

'I'd worked in marketing and advertising for 20 years. Why couldn't I manage to get people through the door to buy a simple cup of coffee?

'But honestly I don't think there's an answer to the question. There are so many reasons why it might not work, and for me it wasn't possible to figure them out.'

Surprised by staff

Neill's biggest surprise was the difficulty he had attracting customers. But his second biggest surprise was staffing: he was astonished by the trouble he had finding reliable staff.

'I was shocked by staff not caring about their job,' said Neill. 'Even though the staff were great most of the time, they didn't care about the job like I did.

'I had times when staff just didn't turn up for their shifts. I'd have a shop full of people wanting coffee, and I'd have to handle it alone because someone hadn't turned up for a shift.

'I made a few mistakes with staff and employed people who couldn't do the job properly. But they didn't stay long. Most of the staff I employed were good at what they did.

'But the unreliability of staff drove me crazy. I just never knew when someone was going to fail to turn up. It made it impossible for me to plan ahead.'

Becoming confident with coffee

Neill had never made coffee before opening Haven Espresso.

'I did a barista course the week before I opened,' said Neill. 'I made sure I employed someone with good barista skills, then I worked alongside them and learned as we went. It took me about a month to become really confident.

'Because making coffee is a technical skill, I enjoyed learning it. I didn't worry about latte art. But I enjoyed figuring out the grind, adjusting it each day, getting the timing right and texturing the milk. The technical side of it made sense to me.'

Neill was determined to make Haven Espresso a haven for great coffee.

'Having consistently good coffee was at the core of everything we did,' said Neill. 'I was always happy with the quality of our coffee. We had great suppliers and I was confident we made coffee very well.

'We sold simple food – toasted sandwiches, slices, cakes, and muffins – and terrific coffee.'

Neill believes that great coffee has more to do with the barista's skill than the quality of the beans.

'We used a local coffee supplier,' said Neill. 'I thought they had a great product, but I'm not persuaded that the brand of coffee makes a big difference to the quality of the coffee. I'm also not sure the brand affects whether people come to the cafe.

'It's how you make the coffee that matters, and the quality of service you offer. I don't believe we would have done any better if we'd had a well-known brand of coffee.'

Not covering costs

Neill's cafe didn't ever get busy enough to cover its costs.

'The income was always inconsistent,' said Neill. 'I never knew when we might have a busy day. There always seemed to be reasons why it might be busy or quiet, but really they were all just guesses.

'I never knew when people might come in, and it made it impossible to plan.'

After a few months of operation, the cafe was busy enough to cover its basic running costs, but it wasn't generating an income for Neill.

'We sold enough to cover the rent, electricity, coffee, milk, and food,' said Neill. 'Sometimes we sold enough to pay for the staff. But sometimes I had to pay the staff out of my own pocket. And it didn't ever pay me.'

Neill tried adjusting his staffing and his opening hours to make the cafe successful.

'Most days I had another staff member on in the mornings,' said Neill. 'That person would go home at about 11 o'clock, and I'd do the rest of the day by myself.

'Initially I opened for seven days a week. But it didn't take me long to realise that was stupid. I wanted to be open every day because I didn't want to miss the money coming in, but I just couldn't keep up the pace. I cut back to six days a week, and closed on Mondays.'

Working multiple jobs

Neill took on extra work to help cover his mounting costs.

'I had a mortgage to pay, so I had no choice,' said Neill. 'At the time I was building my dream house, which was a massive amount of stress itself. I needed to generate an income, and the cafe wasn't providing it.

'I took on night-packing work at a supermarket to stay afloat. And I did some marketing work for an insurance company.

'I was working in the cafe pretty much every hour it was open, plus doing the extra jobs, and trying to supervise my house build. It was crazy, and eventually I realised I couldn't sustain it. I like to work hard, but I couldn't keep working that hard.

'In the end I had a choice: lose my house or sell the business. Choosing between my new house and the business was actually easy. I decided to sell the business and I was fortunate enough to sell it quickly. I put it up for sale just 18 months after opening.

'I was able to sell it for a reasonable amount, pay my debts, and move on. The person who bought it from me seems to be making a go of it: more than three years after I sold, she's still operating under the same name.'

Neill believes the new owner is able to keep afloat because she operates the business alone with no extra staff, and without the added pressure of a mortgage and children.

What is success?

Neill recognises that his cafe wasn't a success, but he's not ready to call it a failure either.

'If being a success means making money, then I guess it wasn't successful,' said Neill. 'But it's not that simple.

'I'm proud of what I did. I created something that wasn't there before. I brought a new business to the area. I created a lovely space, and I was proud of it. A lot of people enjoyed being there. I felt good about it.

'I honestly think it was successful in every way except financial. If I could take money out of the equation, then I'd say it was a great success.'

Would he do it again?

Neill now works for an employer and is enjoying some financial stability. But he doesn't rule out the idea of opening another cafe.

'I don't have any regrets at all. If I had the money and I didn't need to worry about breaking even, I'd definitely do it again. I'd do it tomorrow. I loved having a cafe. I loved the art gallery side of the business. I loved working there. I just wish it had been financially successful.'

But Neill's advice to other potential cafe owners is less optimistic.

'I would say to anyone who is thinking of opening a cafe: don't do it. Anyone wanting to open a cafe needs a lot of money behind them – at least six months of wages and running costs.

'Running a cafe is not the slow-paced dream I thought it would be. It's really, really hard work. It's a poor way to earn money.

'Having your own business is always risky. You've got no security of income. You can't have sick days. If you take a holiday, you won't get paid. You don't know if the work will be consistent.

'And in a cafe it's worse because there are always expenses.

NEWBIES IN THE CAFE

'But even with all the problems, I still think it's a great business if you can find a way to make money.'

Chapter 11

From the university to the cafe and back again

Newbie: Kylie Turville

Cafe: Wares, Plants 'n' Things, Linton Vic (2016 – 2019)

Previous occupation: University lecturer

NEWBIES IN THE CAFE

Before Kylie Turville became a cafe owner, she had a long-term career lecturing in Information Technology at Federation University in Ballarat.

But in 2015, after 16 years of lecturing, Kylie resigned from the university and went looking for adventure. She soon found herself running a cafe and gift shop in the rural town of Linton.

In 2019, less than four years after the adventure began, Kylie made the difficult decision to close the cafe and return to university work. Even though she loved the cafe, she had lost the energy to work the long hours and for a poor income.

Deciding to change careers

Kylie's career took a turn towards the cafe industry when she decided it was time to leave university teaching.

'I'd been in the university system for a long time, and I desperately needed a change,' said Kylie.

'I'd been through several university restructures, and I was finding it impossible to juggle everything in my life. I was working full-time, raising a family, and trying to finish a PhD. It was all too much, and I was in a really bad spot.

'I tried taking long-service leave, and I tried teaching part-time. But I realised I needed a complete break.

'Looking back, it seems crazy that I thought having a cafe would give me a quieter life.'

The perfect location

While Kylie was thinking about possible alternatives to university teaching, she and her husband bought an old shop in the country town of Linton, about 32 km from Ballarat.

'We fell in love with the place,' said Kylie. 'It's a beautiful shop in a gorgeous town, and we thought that renovating it would be a perfect project for us.

'At first we thought we might open a B&B at the back of the building and renovate the shop fronts on the main street. Linton didn't have a B&B, so it seemed like a good option. For us it was a bit of a hobby. We did most of the renovating ourselves, with my parents' help.'

Opening a gift shop

With the renovation underway and her university career behind her, Kylie decided to open a small gift and nursery shop in Linton.

'My idea was to have a little shop that I could operate on my own, with the help of my parents,' said Kylie. 'I was after a complete change of pace, and I wanted something small, with reasonably short hours. I decided to sell gifts and plants.'

Kylie assessed the shops already in Linton and decided that a gift shop would be a good fit.

'The town had some antique shops, a cafe, a takeaway food shop, and a pub. I wanted to do something different – something that would add to what was already available and bring more people to the town. And I really didn't want to open in competition to the existing shops.

'When we opened the gift shop, a cafe was the last thing on my mind. I thought my gift shop would be a hobby and I thought the B&B would bring in enough income to cover the building's cost. But you could say that things didn't go according to plan!'

The accidental cafe

Kylie opened her gift shop, Wares, Plants 'n' Things, in January 2016. But her plan of a quiet shop with limited hours didn't last for long.

Within weeks of Kylie opening the doors, Linton's only cafe closed. And for Kylie, that presented a clear opportunity.

'Everyone we spoke to said that Linton needed a cafe,' said Kylie. 'We agreed, and the solution seemed obvious. We decided to add a cafe to our gift shop. We put our B&B plans on hold, and opened a cafe instead. We've always described ourselves as "accidental" cafe owners.

'I initially thought we'd keep the cafe quite small. My plan was to sell just coffee and cake, and to keep limited hours. But when we opened the cafe, everything changed. It took over.'

Planning a cafe

Kylie and her husband were complete newbies to the cafe industry. They were both university lecturers, with little experience in hospitality. And because the cafe was unplanned, they didn't even have a general vision of the place they wanted to create.

'I'd worked in a commercial kitchen when I was a student,' said Kylie. 'But that was the extent of our combined experience. We really didn't have any idea about what we were doing. Thankfully, we were able to get some really good advice.'

Kylie worked with the local council to understand how to renovate the shop to the standard needed for a food business.

'Because it was an old building, it wasn't feasible to renovate the entire place to meet commercial standards,' said Kylie. 'But it wasn't too difficult to get the kitchen and serving area to comply.

'The people from the council were enormously helpful. They explained exactly what we needed to do.

'I contacted a local catering supplier, and they helped us understand what equipment we needed. We got nearly everything second hand.

'When we opened, we had a 60 centimetre electric domestic oven and a sandwich maker that I bought in Target. We didn't even have a dishwasher! Eventually we bought a commercial dishwasher and I couldn't believe the difference it made. Now I can't believe that we ever operated without one – it really is an essential piece of equipment. But we didn't know that at the time, and somehow we made it work.'

Chapter 11: From the university to the cafe and back again

Planning the business

Kylie and her husband entered the coffee industry with no advance planning or research.

'The cafe was just an opportunistic response to what the town needed,' said Kylie. 'And because it happened that way, we didn't do any initial research. It just seemed like a good idea, so we made it happen.

'And because I thought it was a hobby, I didn't do a business plan or anything like that. It might have been better if I had done a business plan. I don't have a business background at all, so it probably would have been a big help.

'A few things about running a cafe came as a complete surprise to me. I didn't realise there were licensing fees. And I didn't anticipate the impact of collecting GST. Employing staff was harder than I expected. And it goes without saying that the work was harder than I expected!

'We just figured it out as we went along. We also did some reading about the industry and joined a few Facebook groups. The Facebook groups were quite helpful, particularly with things like how to figure out our pricing. It was on a Facebook group that I learned a really useful rule of thumb about pricing – that the menu prices should be 3.3 times the ingredients cost.

'Over time we became a bit more savvy, and I made my own spreadsheets to keep track of income and expenses. But if I'd planned it in advance it probably would have been easier.'

Kylie estimates that it took her a full year to understand the cafe businesses, and another year to feel confident.

'By the time we'd been open for two years, I had a lot of processes and systems in place. By then I knew what I was doing and I wasn't terrified by the work. But I was also starting to feel pretty exhausted by the long hours.'

Learning how to run a cafe

Kylie describes her start in the cafe world as 'slightly insane'.

'When we opened, my coffee-making skills were zilch,' she said. 'My husband and I watched YouTube videos and did some reading online. We got lessons from the person we'd contracted to service our coffee machine, which we bought second hand. But that was about the extent of it. We knew very little.

'At first it was petrifying every time we sold something. But the locals were forgiving and very supportive. They wanted us to succeed because they wanted a cafe in town. So we learned as we went along and asked our customers for lots of feedback.

'I remember being terrified for those first few weeks. People would ask for all sorts of special things, and I had trouble keeping track of the orders. I wasn't at all confident about what I was doing.

'Thankfully I wasn't doing all the baking when we first opened. We made most things on site, but it was some time before I was doing the cooking. I was able to build my cooking skills gradually. These days I can make a perfect breakfast, including poached eggs, and fabulous sweets, including real vanilla slice.

'We started with a very simple menu. But we built it up over the years, as people asked us to do different things. By the time we closed, we were offering full meals with most things made from scratch.'

One of Kylie's early concerns was charging people for the food she'd cooked herself. It took a long time for her to feel comfortable about taking money for her cooking.

'I understand that a cafe is a business and it's got to make money,' said Kylie. 'But it felt wrong to charge money for my cooking. I'm not a chef. There's nothing special about my cooking skills. I'm used to cooking for a family, and they don't pay!

'I found it really difficult to put a price on my food. I always wondered how people could pay so much for my cooking.

'We had some customers who clearly knew a lot about the industry, and they were very supportive. One customer was an event organiser in Melbourne, and he knew a lot about food. He loved our caramel slice and vanilla slice, and that helped to build my confidence.

Chapter 11: From the university to the cafe and back again

'But if I'm honest, that fear about charging for my food never really went away. I always worried that my food wasn't good enough. And I always thought we charged too much for something that I'd cooked.'

Owner-operators who don't take an income

Wares, Plants 'n' Things didn't take long to start paying its own way. Kylie was able to pay the wages, pay the bills on time, and keep up to date with her BAS payments. Owning the building helped, because she viewed the building as an investment, not an expense for the cafe.

But having the cafe pay its own way didn't include paying an income to the owner-operators. Kylie and her husband both worked long hours in the cafe, and they never earned a cent for their work.

'We paid everyone except ourselves,' said Kylie. 'I know that business advisors say cafe owners should pay themselves properly. I know it makes sense to take a wage, not just the profits. But that's easier said than done.

'The reality of small business is that if there's no money left, the owners don't get paid. Everyone else has to be paid first, because without that the business can't operate.

'We couldn't choose whether to pay our staff. But we could choose whether or not to pay ourselves. And the only way to stay open was to not pay ourselves.

'We were fortunate because we were financially secure. My husband kept his full-time job at the university, so we had money coming in. We weren't worried about the future, because we both had good superannuation from our university jobs. So we were in a position to take the financial risk and have me not earning much.'

Working outside the cafe

Even though Kylie wasn't overly concerned about financial security, she did need to earn an income. After one year of working full-time in the cafe, she decided to find part-time work and have the cafe fully staffed.

'The business reality was that I could make more money doing consulting or teaching, so it made sense to pay for cafe staff during the week. On weekends, when staff costs are higher and the cafe was busier, my husband and I worked in the cafe.'

That decision meant both Kylie and her husband were juggling multiple jobs. They worked together in the cafe most Saturdays and Sundays, with Kylie cooking the meals and her husband making coffee. Kylie's husband worked full-time as a lecturer. And Kylie juggled the cafe with contract work.

'It felt as though the cafe was our side interest or hobby,' said Kylie. 'We worked in it for free. And we worked in other jobs during the week to make enough money to keep going.

'I often wondered whether it would be a better decision to leave my paid work and operate the cafe myself. Instead of paying a staff member, I could pay myself.

'But the reality is that I can earn more doing other work, so it made financial sense to employ someone to run the cafe. And the physical work of being in the cafe is much harder than teaching or consulting.'

A planned close

In early 2019, Kylie decided she'd had enough of her cafe lifestyle.

'We were a very small business, with just over $200,000 in annual turnover,' said Kylie. 'But the amount of work and effort involved in generating that turnover was enormous.

'I was busting my gut, working really hard. And at the end of the quarter I'd look at the accounts and see that I'd made nothing. I'd done all that work and it was for nothing. My work–life balance was rubbish.

'Then a few things happened at once, and closing seemed like the best decision.

Chapter 11: From the university to the cafe and back again

'When I reflected on how we were living, our decisions just didn't stack up. My husband and I were hardly seeing our children. We saw each other at work, but we didn't have any family time together. We couldn't even take a holiday, because we were working every weekend.'

Kylie's tipping point came when she was offered a permanent job, her two key staff gave notice, and another cafe opened nearby.

'I was offered a job at the university in a non-teaching role,' said Kylie. 'It's four days a week, which is perfect for me. And it's a great opportunity for me to do an interesting job. It was too good an opportunity to refuse.

'Then we had two staff give us notice. One was having a baby mid-year, and the other was about to finish studying and was looking for work as a counsellor.

'Then, to really help with my decision, another cafe opened in town. I knew what an impact that would have on us.'

Kylie had already had one experience of another cafe opening nearby, and its impact was enormous.

'When another cafe opened in town a few years ago, most of our customers said they wanted to support us both and see us both thrive,' said Kylie. 'But supporting us both didn't mean they spent more money. It simply meant they spread their money between the two cafes. It created a huge drop in our income.

'The other cafe only stayed open a few months, and we soon recovered our trade. But history was repeating itself, and I knew our cafe would take a hit.

'Suddenly it didn't seem to be worth it anymore. We decided to trade until the end of June and then close.'

Closing not selling

Kylie decided not to try selling the cafe. Instead, she simply closed the doors.

'I'd just had enough,' said Kylie. 'I wanted it to end, and I didn't want to do the work involved in selling it.

'I was concerned that selling it would take several months, and I didn't have the energy to keep going.

'We kept trading until the end of June, which was when our manager was starting her maternity leave and I was starting my new job. Then we closed the doors.

'Now with the cafe closed, we can decide what to do with the shop. We might try selling it. Or we might even go back to our original idea and open a B&B.

'I'm back working for an employer, earning a decent income, getting holidays, getting sick pay, and building my superannuation. Within a few weeks of being closed, I realised that I was sleeping better and feeling less stressed. And our house is much tidier!'

Reflecting on the cafe experience

Kylie doesn't have any regrets about the time she spent owning a cafe, but she's not in any hurry to do it again.

'I don't regret it at all,' said Kylie. 'It's something I really wanted to do, and I was fortunate enough to be able to try it for a while. But I've done it now, and I know I don't want to keep doing it.

'I think it's a very difficult industry to make a living in. I wonder whether being in a country town makes it even harder. People seem to think they should pay less in the country, but our costs are exactly the same and sometimes even higher.

'It's such a complicated industry. There are so many aspects to it, and so many pressures. It's an endless cycle, with no relief.

'I wouldn't recommend cafe ownership to anyone who wasn't absolutely passionate about it.'

Even though Kylie doesn't want another cafe for herself, she isn't pessimistic about the industry as a whole.

'I think there's good potential to earn money from a cafe, particularly if it's located in the right area,' she said. 'But in a small country

Chapter 11: From the university to the cafe and back again

town you're quite dependent on what happens in the rest of the community. And while we had the cafe, six or seven different businesses have opened and closed in Linton. It's tough for any business, not just for a cafe.'

It's the people side of the cafe business that Kylie misses the most.

'I made some very good friends in the cafe, and I really enjoyed seeing them regularly,' said Kylie. 'It was a friendly place, and I liked the atmosphere we created.

'What I don't miss is the pressure: the pressure of serving multiple meals at one time, the pressure of the long hours, and the endless pressure to make money.'

'We love living in Linton and having the cafe meant that we got to know so many people. Our cafe became like a community hub. People got to know each other there. That part of it was really beautiful. I'm proud when I think back about what we created.'

The logo for Anthea Williams's Keswick Cafe

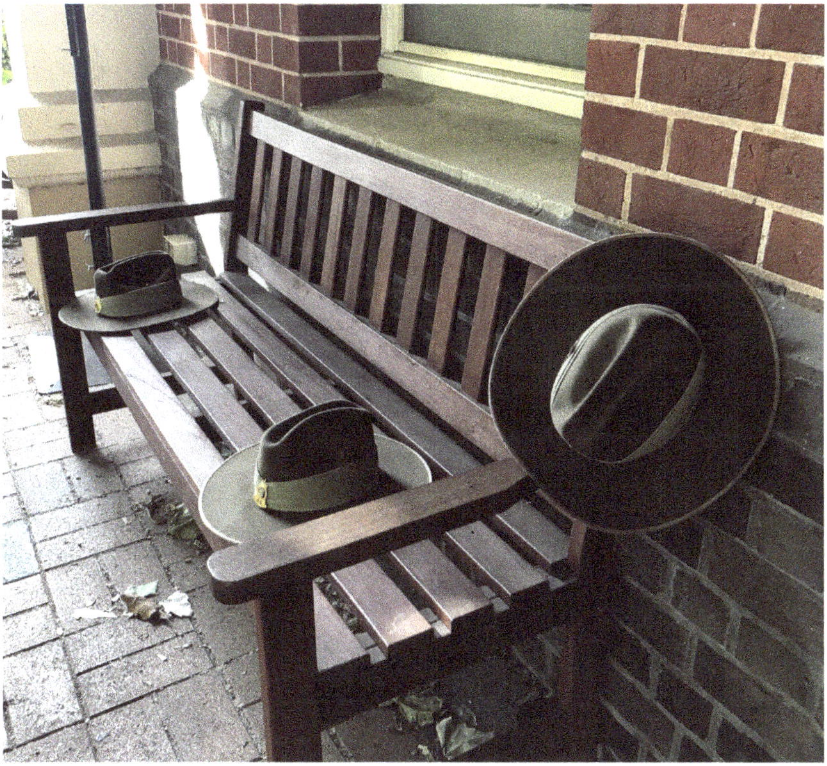

Hats stay outside at Keswick Cafe within Adelaide's Keswick Barracks (Photo: Anthea Williams)

*Keswick Cafe's resident assistance-dog-in-training, Bonnie
(Photo: Anthea Williams)*

Inside Reg James's cafe Bay21 in Forest Hill (Photo: Reg James)

Bay21 latte samples – matcha, beetroot, and turmeric (Photo: Reg James)

The entrance to Reg James's cafe Bay21 in an office park in Forest Hill (Photo: Reg James)

The logo for Neill Hooper's Haven Espresso

Neill Hooper with Penny McKay and a photo of Penny at Haven Espresso's exhibition by Milyjane Photography (Photo: Haven Espresso staff)

Art exhibition at Neill Hooper's cafe Haven Espresso in Stafford Heights (Photo: Neill Hooper)

Inside Neill Hooper's cafe Haven Espresso in Stafford Heights (Photo: Neill Hooper)

The logo for Kylie Turville's Wares, Plants 'n' Things in Linton

Lemon-coconut cake at Kylie Turville's cafe Wares, Plants 'n' Things in Linton (Photo: Kylie Turville)

Barista Chris (who is also Kylie's husband) at Kylie Turville's cafe Wares, Plants 'n' Things in Linton (Photo: Belinda Paul)

Country Heart logo on the front window of Narelle Adams's cafe in Mooroolbark (Photo: Sam McCulloch)

Narelle Adams behind the espresso machine at Country Heart Cafe in Mooroolbark (Photo: Sam McCulloch)

Bringing the country to the city at Narelle Adams's Country Heart Cafe in Mooroolbark (Photo: Sam McCulloch)

Inside Narelle Adams's Country Heart Cafe in Mooroolbark (Photo: Sam McCulloch)

Chapter 12

For the love of people

Newbie: Narelle Adams

Cafe: Country Heart, Coldstream and Mooroolbark Vic (2014 –)

Previous occupation: Childcare worker and student

It was a passion for people that set Narelle Adams on the path to cafe ownership. That, and a love for the family farm.

She's managed to combine them both into her business Country Heart – a cafe, coffee-caravan, and farm-wedding venue in Victoria's Yarra Valley.

And while Narelle might change her business offerings in the years ahead, she's confident about one thing: hospitality and events are where she belongs.

An obvious career choice for a people person

Throughout her school years, Narelle had no idea what career to pursue.

'I was a classic high schooler, with no idea about what to do next,' said Narelle. 'I tried working in childcare for a while. And while I enjoyed that, it didn't feel quite right for me.

'What I really wanted was to own my own business. I knew that it would involve working with people. I just didn't know what business it should be!'

Narelle decided that a business qualification would help her decide on a career choice, so she enrolled in the Bachelor of Business at Swinburne University of Technology. While she was studying, she landed on the idea for her first business, a coffee-caravan called Frankie.

'I decided to enrol at uni because I thought people would take me more seriously if I had a degree,' said Narelle. 'I'm conscious that I'm young and don't have a lot of experience.

'There were definitely times when I was first operating Frankie that I struggled. I'd be talking to suppliers and I felt they were looking down on me as a young female newbie. But when I said I was studying at uni, their attitude seemed to change.

'I think the degree set me up really well with a basic understanding of how businesses run, how the financial side of things works, and how to negotiate. It gave me a lot of confidence.'

Chapter 12: For the love of people

The beginning of a dream

While Narelle was studying, she found information online about cafes located in old buses and trams.

'I can't tell you how excited I was when I found those images,' said Narelle. 'On our family farm, we've got some beautiful old buses. I started to dream about how I could convert the buses into a cafe, and have a cafe on our farm.

'I did some research, and quickly realised that a bus conversion was out of my reach. It would be a complicated and expensive project.

'But as I looked around, I found photographs of converted caravans, and that seemed like a much more do-able project.

'I decided that a coffee-caravan would make a great first business for me. At first it was a side project with a friend, but it soon became my full-time passion.'

Setting up Frankie, the coffee-caravan

Narelle had no experience in the coffee industry and knew nothing about how to refurbish a caravan. But she wasn't about to let that stop her following her dream. With her parents' help she bought a 1970s Franklin caravan, and started to think about the fitout.

'I worked with my close friend from university, Erin, to get Frankie up and running,' said Narelle. 'At first we ran it jointly. Erin had a background in hospitality and I had the business focus, so we made a good team.

'Erin and I did a lot of research to understand the workflow and decide where everything should go. We thought about what angle to have the coffee machine on, how we'd serve customers, and where everything would be kept. It's a tiny space, so it was important to get it right.

'The caravan is a bit different to a normal cafe setup, because it has to be able to run on domestic power or a generator. We can't have one of the big double-boiler espresso machines.'

In 2014, with the caravan conversion complete, Narelle and Erin set up shop outside Narelle's family farm, on the side of the Maroondah Highway near Coldstream in the Yarra Valley. They named their business Country Heart because they wanted a name that connected them to the Yarra Valley and left their options open for future business expansion.

They sold coffee on weekday mornings, when the highway was at its busiest. They also started to attend local markets and, before long, took bookings for private events.

Finding her passion

With Frankie the coffee-caravan, Narelle found her career of passion. 'As soon as I started operating Frankie, I knew that hospitality was the right industry for me. I loved it straight away.

'I love everything about it. I love getting to know people when they buy coffee. I love the way that food and coffee can bring people together. For me, that's what hospitality is all about: bringing people together.'

But getting started wasn't without its difficulties and lessons. Narelle found herself on a steep learning curve.

'Getting into the coffee industry was a huge thing for me. I had so much to learn. Erin had a lot of experience, and she was a great support. I've got other friends who've worked in cafes, and they helped me a lot. I also found a great coffee supplier who was very patient with me.

'When I look back now on those early days in 2014, I think I must have been serving some terrible coffee! I was fortunate to have a forgiving blend of beans and a supplier who was willing to train me well.

'I think the novelty of Frankie helped to build interest. People seemed to love the idea of buying coffee from a converted caravan. It's great to be able to pull up at markets and events and set up shop.'

Chapter 12: For the love of people

At first, Narelle and Erin worked together in the business. 'We worked really well together,' said Narelle. 'But after about a year, we made the tough decision to part ways. Erin couldn't financially contribute to building the business, and she decided to move on to a career in HR.'

Most days, Narelle worked alone in Frankie and kept her overheads low. Her weekly morning coffee trade was enough to cover operating costs, and her weekend work at markets and functions provided her with some profit.

'Being a sole operator made it relatively easy to control my costs,' said Narelle. 'Sometimes it was busy enough for me to bring on a second person, and that's when my costs grew quickly. I had to be really careful to be sure I could justify that person's wage.'

Support from family and friends

Narelle had a lot of help from family and friends to get her business off the ground. Her parents helped with funding, her mother baked cakes and slices for her to sell, and her friends and sisters often worked for free.

'I couldn't have done it without their generous support,' said Narelle. 'In the first year, I couldn't even tow Frankie myself. I had a tiny car, so my dad and my (now) husband used to tow the van to events.

'Eventually we traded my little car and upgraded so that I could tow it myself. That brought new challenges, because I had to learn how to tow.

'The very first event I towed myself to, I forgot to take Frankie's brake off when I left to come home. The brake caught fire while I was towing, and it was just me and my sister in the car! A wonderful person with a fire extinguisher stopped and helped us!

'We were driving home for my engagement party, and we managed to get a tow truck to collect Frankie and get it home and ready in time to serve drinks for our party! I learned my lesson about checking brakes that night!'

A wedding, and new opportunities

When Narelle got married in 2016, her wedding was held on the family farm.

'As we planned our own wedding, we realised that we have a magnificent venue available to us,' said Narelle. 'Our wedding was featured on a wedding blog, and people started to contact us about hiring the farm as a venue.

'That sparked my next dream: I decided to set up the farm as a wedding venue.'

In 2017, Narelle applied to the local council for a permit to hold weddings and events at the farm. The approval took over a year to come through. While she was waiting, Narelle returned to childcare.

'I loved working in Frankie, but it wasn't really a full-time job,' said Narelle. 'I thought it was time for me to earn a proper adult income, so I went back to childcare a few days a week and operated Frankie on the other days.'

Opportunity knocks again

While Narelle was (im)patiently waiting for council approval for her farm-weddings plan, she found a run-down cafe for sale in the Melbourne suburb of Mooroolbark. It was an opportunity too good to miss.

'I'd been wanting a fixed cafe rather than just the van,' said Narelle. 'I wanted to be able to do more and I was really keen to employ staff.

'I knew that I wanted to have a cafe on the farm one day, but I wasn't sure whether it would be feasible and I thought I should get more experience first. So when this cafe came on the market, I bought it.'

Chapter 12: For the love of people

Even though Narelle's cafe is in the suburbs of Melbourne, it's only 15 minutes from the family farm.

'The cafe was quite run down and had been run by a couple with no extra staff,' said Narelle.

'I thought it looked like a good investment for someone without a lot of experience. It's a great location, opposite the train station. And looking through the bookwork I felt confident that I could improve the previous owner's turnover.'

Getting the cafe established

Narelle opened Country Heart Cafe in October 2017 and, within the first week had doubled the average takings of the previous owners.

She opened without a formal business plan, but with a clear vision in her mind of what she was doing. Her only formal planning was a financial forecast, which she feels wasn't particularly helpful.

'I didn't write a formal business plan, but I did do a lot of informal planning,' said Narelle. 'I did everything you'd normally do for a business plan – like a SWOT analysis and market research – but I didn't write any of it down.

'I didn't need to present a business plan to anyone, so I don't think that writing one would have helped me. I'm not really the type of person to keep referring to a written plan. I use a spreadsheet to keep track of things, and that's enough.

'I wish I'd done a more accurate financial forecast though. I based my figures on data the previous owners provided and on the industry standards provided by government, and they weren't very accurate. There were a lot of hidden costs I didn't expect.

'Because it was my first cafe, I didn't know enough about all the costs involved. Now, after operating for two years, I've got a much more accurate financial forecast in place.'

What Narelle lacked in formal planning she made up for with vision. She knew exactly what she wanted the cafe to achieve.

151

'My concept has always been to celebrate the farm,' said Narelle. 'With the cafe, I want to bring a patch of the country into town. Country hospitality is the theme of the fitout and our menu.

'We make our food on site, and we want it to be the type of food you'd find on a country farm. We often get people telling us that their nana used to make food like ours. It's exactly what I want to hear!'

Unexpected challenges

Establishing the cafe wasn't without its surprises. For Narelle, the biggest surprises were staff costs and the impact of GST.

'I'd been so keen to employ people, but I hadn't anticipated all the on-costs that come with it,' said Narelle. 'It's so much more than the hourly rate. And while I understood that in theory, the reality of it was very hard.

'The industry standard suggests that wages should be around 35 per cent of turnover. But I find that very difficult to achieve. I pay award wages and do everything by the books because I decided before I opened that I wanted to run my business properly. But my wages usually sit at about 45 per cent of turnover, which is really too high. And that's without me taking an income for the hours I work.

'The other thing I hadn't anticipated was the way GST works. Again, I understood it on paper, but the reality was a surprise.

'Because we make our food on site, we don't pay GST on ingredients, but we collect GST on everything we sell. It adds up so quickly and the first BAS was a big shock. It made me assess how feasible it is to make things from scratch.

'I wish I'd known to put aside money for the BAS right from day one. The first quarter took me by surprise and I wasn't prepared. It's so easy to let yourself get behind, and catching up is really hard.

'I still find the financial side of the business the most difficult. I've got a brilliant bookkeeper, and she helps me to keep track of everything. But the pricing is hard.

Chapter 12: For the love of people

'Because we make most things from scratch, I try to keep our ingredients cost at 25 per cent of the sale price. But that's not always possible because I can't let the sale price get too high. We have to make our pricing competitive, so I focus a lot on controlling our costs.'

As Narelle settled into cafe ownership, she re-thought her opening hours and looked for ways to cut costs.

'We initially operated seven days a week,' said Narelle. 'But I soon realised that Sundays aren't feasible. The costs of opening just didn't add up.

'Being open six days is manageable. I'm in the cafe five days a week and I've got flexibility about taking time off when I've got an event to run. I don't need to be there every day, and I don't need to be in the cafe for crazy-long hours.'

Weddings at the farm

Just as Narelle was opening the cafe, she received council approval to run 10 events at the farm every year.

'At first I thought that 10 events wouldn't be enough,' said Narelle. 'But now I realise that it's just about perfect.

'Offering just 10 dates a year helps to keep our venue a bit exclusive, and it means that we can choose dates to suit us and the farm. It also means I can operate it as a hobby.'

Narelle's family farm is a working farm, complete with sprouts, cabbages, tractors, and cows (plus those abandoned buses). It's around 800 acres, with the extended family all living onsite in separate houses.

Narelle has established the farm as a BYO venue for weddings. Guests get exclusive access to the farm, and organise their own catering and equipment. Over time, Narelle plans to build her facilities.

'At the moment it's a pretty basic venue,' said Narelle. 'The landscape is absolutely stunning, but it's definitely a venue within a working farm.

'In 2018 we installed permanent toilets, so we no longer have to rely on portaloos. In 2019 we bought some rustic trestle tables, which we had made specially for us. Over time I'd like to improve the events shed and get a marquee for outdoor weddings.

'It's a very simple, honest venue, and that's the way I want to keep it. We're offering people a real working farm in the most beautiful of environments. And people seem to really love it.

'We've already had a huge range of events and styles – everything from food trucks and grazing tables to spit roasts and formal sit-down dinners.

'I've discovered that I absolutely love the wedding and events industry. I'm doing something wonderful and creative in a location that I absolutely love. I'm confident that our events can fit alongside other parts of my life.'

Consistent branding

Narelle operates her cafe, Frankie the coffee-caravan, and the farm weddings under the same brand name: Country Heart. She decided that consistent branding would help with cross promotion.

'By the time I opened the cafe, I already had a small social media following from Frankie,' said Narelle. 'It seemed logical to keep the name the same, and the name fits the theme of everything we do.

'I think the consistent branding is really helping the different businesses to support each other. The wedding market definitely feeds into the cafe. When potential wedding clients see that we've got a cafe, they can come and experience our service.'

Making a living

Like many independent suburban cafes, Narelle's Country Heart Cafe struggles to make a living for its owner. After two years of operation, Narelle is yet to take a proper income.

Chapter 12: For the love of people

'The cafe isn't quite paying for itself yet,' said Narelle. 'My biggest question is how to bring more people through the door. We have a number of competitors close by, and I think they make it difficult.

'I work in the cafe five days a week, and I don't take any income from it. All the income I make comes from events and Frankie.'

But for Narelle, the events and Frankie are like hobbies. They're what she does on the weekends, and the cafe is her core business.

'I can see that the cafe is growing and it's definitely getting closer to being profitable,' said Narelle. 'The days that we used to consider busy when we opened two years ago are like our quiet days now. But we're not quite there yet, and it makes it so hard to keep going.'

After two years of trade, Country Heart Cafe is selling around 16 kilograms of coffee each week. Narelle estimates that 20 kilograms a week would give her a reasonable income, and has set 25 kilograms as a longer-term goal.

'We're so close!' said Narelle. 'But the reality for me is that we're not quite there. That little bit of extra income would make all the difference.'

Achieving profitability is proving more difficult than Narelle expected, but she loves every other aspect of owning a cafe.

'Having the cafe has been a hugely positive experience for me,' said Narelle. 'I love it. But I'm feeling a bit stumped about what to do next. I can't continue indefinitely without an income.

'I've been married a few years, and we're keen to start a family. But I can't figure out how to have a family when I spend so many hours in the cafe.

'The problem is the income. If we were busier, I'd be able to afford to pay someone else to work the hours I'm currently doing. But right now I can't see how to make it work financially.

'I recognise that you have to be in this business for the long haul. It takes a long time to build a customer base and I don't think it's unusual to take a few years to become profitable. Building a new cafe doesn't fit very well with wanting to start a family.

'Sometimes I get upset because it looks as though other cafes are succeeding and I wonder whether I'm missing something important. But I tell myself there's not much transparency in this industry. Just because the other cafes look busy, that doesn't mean they're making money.

'I've also wondered whether my lack of experience is showing. Maybe I needed to get more advice and work alongside someone who had been in the business for a while.'

What next?

Narelle isn't sure what the future holds. She's got some difficult decisions ahead about family–work balance.

She's confident that she could juggle three small businesses with a family if they were all bringing in enough income to pay for full staffing. But right now she feels that she can't keep the cafe unless she continues to work in it herself without taking an income.

Whatever decision she makes, one thing is certain: hospitality is her passion, and she's got no plans to change careers.

'I'm excited about my future business ideas, and I've still got a long-term dream of opening a cafe on the farm. I think it would be attractive to tourists – a non-wine offering in the Yarra Valley. I'd do very simple, farm-style food.

'A girl's got to have a dream!'

Chapter 13

Lessons from the newbies

> **In this chapter:** A baker's dozen of lessons from the newbies
>
> **Learnings:** Combined lessons from our stories
>
> **Be confident:** Enjoy your cafe journey!

A baker's dozen of lessons from the newbies

1. Write a business plan only if you plan to use it
2. Do a financial forecast
3. Make sure you understand the impact of GST and PAYG
4. Think carefully before working with your partner, family members, or friends
5. Know how long you can survive without earning an income
6. Have a back-up plan
7. Remember that it's a business, not a tea party
8. Develop a promotion plan
9. Do your research about staffing
10. Get to know the industry
11. Do some 'what if' planning and risk assessment
12. Beware of being so consumed by the work that you lose sight of the vision
13. Develop confidence in what you're doing

Chapter 13: Lessons from the newbies

This chapter includes our top suggestions for the next generation of cafe newbies. It draws on the experiences and challenges faced by the 11 newbies featured in this book to provide practical suggestions for people who are thinking of opening their own cafe.

We know how strong the cafe dream can be, and we won't do anything to persuade you away from cafe ownership. We all believe that successful cafes are not only possible, but are highly achievable. But to make your cafe journey a success, there's some stuff we think you need to know.

Please remember that the suggestions in this chapter are based on the experiences of the people profiled in this book. We're current and former cafe owners, not paid business advisors. We don't understand your particular situation.

What we can offer is realistic advice based on our experiences. We encourage you to support this with advice that's specific to you.

1. Write a business plan only if you plan to use it

Most business advisors will tell you that a business plan is an essential prerequisite for starting a small business. And, if you're planning to borrow money for establishment costs, you'll probably find that a business plan is required as part of the loan application.

A business plan can be an enormously useful document. The process of writing the business plan can help you to think through every aspect of your business. Through the planning, you'll be prompted to consider a range of issues, understand your vision, and set your direction.

But a business plan is only as useful as you make it. A good business plan will guide every decision you make and become a roadmap for your cafe journey. But a poor business plan that doesn't capture your vision or is written in a way that's vague and generic won't help you at all.

When it comes to a business plan:

- If your plan doesn't reflect the specific reality you face, then it's not worth writing
- If you don't refer to it, it's not worth writing
- If you don't regularly update it, it will quickly become useless.

If you already have a clear idea of where you're heading and you're not the type of person to refer to written documents, then you probably won't get any benefit from a written business plan. If this is you and you don't need a business plan to borrow money, it's probably not worth the effort involved in writing one.

How to write a business plan

If you decide to write a business plan, it's best to write it yourself.

It really doesn't matter whether you've got strong writing skills. It doesn't matter whether you understand how formal business documents look. The business plan is for you, and you're the person who needs to understand it. Nobody understands your business like you do, and you're the best person to capture your own vision.

Yes, you might need to discuss your business plan with trusted advisors (some of whom may be paid advisors). Yes, you may decide to employ a writer if you need to provide a business plan for your bank. But the plan should be yours: it needs to capture your detailed ideas for the business and guide every decision you make.

A three-step approach to writing a business plan:

1. Brainstorm ideas and do research – make notes about every aspect of your dream business (cover everything you can think of – what you'll sell, where you'll be located, how you'll figure out pricing, how you'll employ staff, what you want to get out of the business, what your opening hours will be, how you'll promote the cafe, who your competitors are ... nothing is off limits at this stage).
2. Assemble your ideas and make decisions – accept the best of your brainstormed ideas and reject anything that's not feasible. Start to write down your ideas as statements about how you will run the business.

3. Write the business plan – your plan can be as simple as your brainstormed notes assembled into a working document. If you need something more structured, you could download a business plan template and use those headings (most state governments have templates available for free). There's no 'rule' saying the business plan must be written a particular way. But if you're writing the plan for your bank, it's worth asking what they'd like to see.

It's best to start with brainstorming and thinking, not with a business plan template. If you start with the template and then try to create the content the template asks for, there's a good chance you'll worry too much about the template and not enough about what you want to do in your cafe.

I produced a long business plan before I opened my meetings venue and cafe. I've included my section headings in Appendix 1. They worked well for me, and you might find them helpful.

Getting help to write a business plan

If you decide to employ someone to help write your business plan, make sure you work closely with the person writing it. Plenty of people offer 'off-the-shelf' business plans, and their plans are likely to be useless. A generic business plan with a lot of standard wording is unlikely to be a useful guide for you. Make sure that your plan is specific to you and tailored exactly to your needs.

If someone else writes the plan, make sure you read and understand every word. If the plan covers things that you don't understand or you don't plan to do, it's hardly a plan for your business.

Don't just write a start-up plan

A good business plan will go well beyond the fit-out and start-up phases of your cafe. Your business plan should guide everything you do and include every phase of your cafe's development.

It probably makes sense for your first business plan to cover the start-up and initial phase of operation (perhaps the first three years).

It also makes sense to revisit and revise that business plan regularly – perhaps every three months in the first year, and every six or twelve months after that.

As your business matures, your business plan will need to mature with it. Your business plan should cover ongoing operations, possible expansion, and your exit strategy.

2. Do a financial forecast

Even if you don't write a business plan, you'll need a financial forecast that helps you understand your likely income and expenses. As part of the financial forecast, it's helpful to understand your sales targets and ratios.

A little research should help you uncover targets and ratios that are reasonable for the type of cafe you plan to operate. If you've got these sorted out before you open, they'll be very useful in helping you assess how you're going. Ideally, you'll be able to look at the takings summary every day and have a very clear idea of what it means for your bottom line.

In Appendix 2 you'll find the sales targets and ratios I worked out for my meetings venue and cafe. These ratios seemed about right for a smallish cafe in the Brisbane suburbs. They may not be the right numbers for you, but they may get you thinking about what you need. I developed them from online research and conversations with suppliers and other cafe owners.

Understand your target income and growth timeline. Then halve it

As part of your financial forecast, you'll figure out your sales targets, your break-even point, and your growth timeline. You need to know these numbers inside out, so that you understand how your cafe is tracking every day and every week.

These calculations will help you understand what turnover you need before the cafe will break even, what turnover will give you an income, and what turnover will allow you to employ more staff.

Chapter 13: Lessons from the newbies

If you understand these numbers before you open, you'll be able to make sensible decisions based on what the numbers say (not based on your exhaustion or fear of failure).

When I researched my business, a coffee supplier told me that viable cafes in the Brisbane suburbs need to sell at least 20 kilograms of coffee each week. The supplier said that most cafes achieve this within three months of operation.

Based on my own experience and my conversations for this book, the 20 kilograms per week target seems about right. What's questionable though, is whether you've got any chance of achieving it within three months.

One story that was common across all the people I spoke to in writing this book was that initial growth was slower than expected and achieving viability took longer than expected. That's why I've suggested you halve your initial target.

If you're starting a new cafe, it's likely to take some time to achieve viability. The combined stories in this book suggest that two or three years might be a realistic time. My cafe reality was that we sold around 11 kilograms of coffee each week, with very slow growth. We got to 11 kilograms reasonably quickly, but moving beyond it proved difficult. We assumed that selling 19 kilograms per week would give us a viable cafe.

3. Make sure you understand the impact of GST and PAYG

When you operate a cafe, it's possible to lose money every week and still face a significant bill for GST and PAYG.

Before you open the doors, make sure you understand exactly how GST (Goods and Services Tax) and PAYG (Pay As You Go income tax) work. Start saving for your tax from day one.

It's really important that you don't get behind on your tax payments. These are debts that will not go away. They continue to build every day your cafe is open.

NEWBIES IN THE CAFE

GST

You'll collect GST on every sale you make. It's one-eleventh of your takings, and you will probably report and pay every quarter. You claim back the GST you paid on the costs of making your income.

So when you pay GST on your rent or your coffee machine maintenance, you claim that money back. But here's the big catch for cafes – there's currently no GST paid on coffee beans, milk, bread, and basic ingredients. So while you'll pay GST (and therefore claim it back) when you purchase a wholesale cake or pie for resale, you won't pay any GST when you buy the ingredients and make the cake or pie yourself. When you're calculating your selling prices, make sure you consider the impact of GST.

If possible, do a rough GST calculation every week, and put aside your GST payment in a separate account. That way you'll be able to pay the GST when it's due. If you can't pay on time, the tax office will let you set up a payment plan. But while you're meeting the payment plan, you still need to be saving for the next GST instalment. Once you get behind, it can be very difficult to catch up.

PAYG and superannuation

When you employ staff, you will collect their PAYG tax and superannuation. You'll usually need to make payments to the tax office and superannuation clearing house each quarter.

Each week's total for PAYG and superannuation might seem small. But over three months, they will add up to several thousand dollars. If you don't put the PAYG and superannuation money aside in a separate account, you might find that you struggle to pay when they fall due – particularly as your payments will coincide with your GST (GST and PAYG are reported and paid together on your Business Activity Statement; superannuation is reported separately).

4. Think carefully before working with your partner, family members, or friends

Don't assume that working with your partner/family/friends will be easy because you already know them. Working with people you know has the potential to be a disaster. You might find yourself with a ruined relationship or find yourself choosing between the business and the relationship.

If you decide to go into business with someone you know, consider getting an independent advisor to help you set up a written agreement with an exit strategy. If you do this, you may find you're able to keep your relationship even if you part ways in business.

Some couples, family members, and friends work together brilliantly (and you'll find some of their stories in this book). But many people are not so lucky: they find themselves in situations they didn't anticipate, unsure what to do or how to change, and unable to talk about it in an objective, rational, emotion-free way.

If you decide to go into business with your partner, family members, or friends, make sure you:

- Have an open conversation before starting the business (if you can't talk about possible issues before the business opens, there's little chance you'll be able to have a constructive conversation if problems arise)
- Jointly participate in the business planning so you share a common vision
- Write a formal agreement about how the business will operate and who will do what
- Write an exit strategy
- Agree to employ an independent mediator if needed.

These suggestions apply mostly to business partnerships, and particularly to couples who decide to work together. But deciding to employ family and friends (or their children) is an equally important decision. If you employ family and friends, make sure you're very clear about the expectations and whether they'll be treated like every other employee.

5. Know how long you can survive without earning an income

Before you open, think carefully about your financial stability and how long you can survive without an income from the cafe. Many cafe owners never take an income for themselves.

Any business advisor will tell you that you should take an income from your business. They'll even go as far as saying that you shouldn't be in business if you can't take an income for yourself. But this isn't always sound advice. You may decide to give yourself a set amount of time before you need an income. You may decide that you'll make your money when you sell the business. Or your cafe may be a hobby that you're doing for other reasons, and you may not be particularly concerned about your personal income.

Whatever your financial goals, your cafe journey will be less stressful if you have financial security that means you're not dependent on the cafe's income. You're likely to feel more financially secure if your partner has a stable income, you have an income from another source (e.g., investments or superannuation), you have strong savings, you have few living expenses (e.g., no mortgage), or you're able to continue earning money from another source.

If you have reasonable financial security, you'll have a greater chance of supporting yourself until the cafe achieves viability. If you're relying on the cafe to cover your mortgage or support your family in the first year of operation, you may find yourself facing significant financial pressure.

In our business planning, Anne-Maree and I thought we'd be able to survive for three years with little income before we seriously risked our house, mostly because I planned to continue earning money through consulting. That assessment was about right, but we failed to consider the possibility that our business would make continual losses. Because our meeting venue lost money every month and because our growth was slower than anticipated, the financial pressures we faced felt extreme.

The cafe newbies who get most enjoyment from their cafes seem to be those who have financial security that's independent of the cafe. Because they're not relying on the cafe to cover their living expenses within a set timeframe, they're able to enjoy the cafe experience and let it grow at its own pace.

Have cash reserves to keep you going for the early months

Whatever you're doing about financial stability, you'll need cash reserves to cover your set-up costs and initial operating costs.

You'll need money in the bank to cover your initial wages, rent, electricity, and product costs. Your cafe will cost you money every day, whether you sell a coffee of not.

My coffee supplier recommended that I needed cash reserves sufficient to cover these basic costs for three to six months. This was good advice and helped to reduce the pressures we experienced in the initial months of operation. Knowing that we had cash in the bank to pay every bill on time made everything easier, even though our cash reserves weren't being replaced as quickly as we'd hoped.

As your cafe grows, your product, ingredient, and staffing costs will grow too. While each additional sale will improve your ability to break even, additional sales also create additional costs. Paying close attention to your income and expenses can help you manage your cash flow as you grow.

6. Have a back-up plan

Opening a cafe is an exciting, creative adventure. It's also a lot of hard work. Every year, many cafe owners reach their limit and decide to close.

Before you open your cafe, think about:
- How will you know you've reached the point where you need to close?

- What will you do if you reach the point where you need to close?

Every cafe newbie should have a back-up plan ready to be implemented if the need arises. Ideally, it should be written down and ready to go, because when you're stressed you won't be thinking clearly and you may make poor decisions.

Having a back-up plan is particularly important if you've got a lot to lose (e.g., your house) or if you're committed to the cafe premises. If you own the premises or are contracted into a lease, your expenses will not go away simply because you close the doors. You may even find that your lease includes a clause that forces you to trade.

Think creatively as you develop your back-up plan. Your back-up plan might include:
- Using the premises for a different business
- Transferring the lease to a new tenant
- Employing staff to run the cafe while you go back to your previous career
- Going through bankruptcy so you can start again with a clean slate.

Deciding to sell the business is probably not a great back-up plan. Cafes can take several months to sell, and you'll need to keep trading through the marketing and selling process. If you've reached your limit as a cafe owner, operating it while it's on the market may be beyond you.

7. Remember that it's a business, not a tea party

Most cafe newbies are in some way captivated by the cafe dream. You might love coffee and have a passion for food. You might dream about the relaxed pace and welcoming environment you'll create for customers.

Remember that the perfect environment is something you create for your customers. It will not be your everyday experience. As the cafe owner, you are taking on hard work and customer demands.

Your cafe is a business. And for you it needs to be a business first. No matter how much you love to produce excellent coffee and perfect food, those things should take second place to your business needs.

You need to run your cafe with a focus on maximising profitability, increasing turnover, and minimising waste. Coffee, food, customer service, and a welcoming environment are all important. They create the place that customers will flock to. But none of them matter if you can't make the business work.

Don't open a cafe if you're seeking a quieter life

The cafe dream often comes with visions of a quieter life, where you set your own hours, escape from the demands of a boss, and share endless coffees with friends. The cafe reality won't be like that, particularly not if you expect to make money.

There's a reasonable chance you'll be disappointed if you think that a cafe will:

- Be less busy and less demanding than your current industry
- Be easier work than your current industry
- Give you freedoms you don't get as an employee
- Help you achieve a work–life balance
- Give you more time to spend with your family.

When I was planning our cafe, I remember thinking that I couldn't possibly be busier than I already was. I couldn't imagine how a cafe could increase the demands on my time. I was a busy consultant!

I couldn't have been more wrong. Nothing prepared me for the long hours and unforgiving schedule of a 7-day-a-week, 10-hour-a-day operation. Nothing prepared me for the demands of customers and regular opening hours, which made it seem that I was no longer in control of my time. Mind you, I made the same mistake before having children. You'd think I might know better!

Accept that the work is not predictable

Cafe income and cafe customers are unpredictable. It sometimes seems there's inside knowledge shared by customers that makes them all stay away at the same time, then all turn up at the same time. And no one shared that knowledge with you.

It's possible that you'll never develop clear busy days and busy times. This can make rostering and ordering very difficult – and little more than a guessing game.

You're likely to be less stressed if you accept that customers are not predictable and you don't spend too much time trying to second-guess your customer patterns. Sometimes it will be quiet. Sometimes it will be busy. Sometimes there will be a reason for this. But often there won't be. It's best not to over-think it, and just get on with the job.

Start small if you can

You may have big dreams for your cafe – perhaps a large venue, perhaps multiple income streams, perhaps multiple sites.

Whatever your dream, you're most likely to succeed if you can find a way to start small. Starting small will allow you to test your ideas and adapt them as needed. Starting small will also enable you to grow as you can afford it, without taking a huge risk up front.

8. Develop a promotion plan

My research suggests that promotion is a problem for most cafe newbies. Most of the cafe owners I spoke to were disappointed by the number of customers walking through the door. Most discovered that their cafe's growth was slower than expected.

One way to address this problem is to work hard on promotion. Before you open your cafe, spend time thinking about how you will promote the business. Develop a plan that tells you what to do, when.

If possible, use promotion to build a community of followers – people who are interested in what you're doing and want you to succeed. If you begin to build this community before you open, they'll be your initial customers. The best promotion you can get is when your community of supporters encourages their friends to visit your cafe.

Chapter 13: Lessons from the newbies

Identify a clear gap in the market, and promote to that gap
In most Australian towns, customers can choose from many, many cafes. It's a crowded market, with a lot of competition. You need to identify your market and give the market a reason to visit you. Then, you need to make sure they know you exist.

Promote directly to your target market, and don't try to be all things to all people. Try to offer exactly what your target market will want. Promote to that market using the communication tools they recognise.

If you're marketing to local residents, you might find that your best promotion comes from letterbox drops. If you're promoting to small-business people, then it might make sense to offer free wi-fi and join business networking groups. If you're promoting to younger cafe lovers, you'll want to be all over social media (preferably with photos of whatever food is currently on-trend).

In Appendix 3, I've included some suggestions about ways you can promote your cafe. These might be helpful as you put together your own promotion plan.

9. Do your research about staffing

Employing staff adds an additional layer of complexity to your business. When you employ staff, you suddenly need to manage people and personalities, handle rosters and timesheets, and meet your responsibilities as an employer.

If you haven't employed staff before, you'll need to research the relevant awards, working conditions, and employer responsibilities. The relevant information is all freely available on state and federal government websites. If you don't meet your responsibilities as an employer, you run the risk of legal action by your employees.

If possible, plan your approach to employing staff before you open your doors, even if you don't expect to employ staff straight away. By the time you're ready to employ a paid staff member, you'll be so busy that you won't have time to do the research required.

Your decisions about staffing might include whether you'll:
- Employ for skills or personality/fit with your business
- Have rules/guidelines about employee conduct (e.g., how they interact with customers, how they carry food, what decisions they can make without asking you, whether they can mention you on social media)
- Have a uniform or dress code
- Provide training
- Ask staff to contribute to your business planning.

It's best to put together an employment pack for new staff, which might include:
- A form where you collect their details (contact information, banking details, superannuation fund)
- The tax declaration form
- A staff manual that explains your business vision and what they can expect from the job.

In Appendix 4, I've included some headings that you might like to include in your staff manual.

10. Get to know the industry

If you're a cafe newbie, you'll be lacking in hands-on cafe experience. No matter how much reading and cafe-watching you do, nothing can compare to real experience.

If you're serious about the cafe business but you've never worked in hospitality before, it's probably a good idea to try it out before you open your own cafe. You might like to:
- Do a barista course and a food safety supervisor course
- Enrol in a TAFE-level hospitality certificate, which will teach you about the industry and include a work placement
- Find a job in a cafe – preferably a low-level job that will have you clearing tables and washing dishes
- Talk to people who own and operate cafes (or have done so in the past)

Chapter 13: Lessons from the newbies

- Talk to suppliers (including equipment suppliers)
- Get advice from your local council's food licensing team
- Work with an independent cafe coach or business advisor
- Join a cafe networking group (either via social media or a local group that meets face-to-face).

If you're a newbie, you need to be willing to ask questions – lots of them. Ask people you trust about how things work and why things work that way. Ask questions that will let you compare the options and make your own decisions.

When you're researching the industry, it's easy to look through rose-coloured glasses and imagine that your cafe won't experience the problems you identify. We all excel in identifying problems and imagining that we understand exactly how to solve them. We all believe that things will be different for us or that we'll do a better job than everyone else.

Take a long, hard look at every problem you see. Then, instead of assuming you won't experience that problem because your cafe will be different, imagine how you would address that problem to achieve a good outcome.

Work with a cafe coach or business advisor

An independent cafe coach or business advisor who isn't aligned to any product or supplier might be the right person to help you through the start-up phase. A coach or advisor will cost you money, but it's possible that their advice will save you more than it costs.

You may be able to work with a coach or advisor to:
- Develop your cafe vision
- Develop your business plan
- Learn about the industry
- Find premises and secure a lease
- Fit out the cafe and purchase equipment
- Make decisions about how to run the cafe
- Employ and train staff.

A good coach or advisor will be an independent advocate, working for you. They'll put your interests first and not rigidly direct you towards a particular style of business.

It's likely that a cafe or hospitality coach will be more useful to cafe newbies than a general business advisor. Cafe/hospitality coaches should have a detailed understanding of the industry and support you in every decision you make. General business advisors are less likely to have the industry knowledge you need.

11. Do some 'what if' planning and risk assessment

When you're planning your cafe, challenge yourself with as many 'what if' questions as possible. If you've thought these things through in advance, you'll know what to do if they happen. You'll also save yourself from having to make quick decisions when you're feeling stressed and overwhelmed. The more you prepare before you open, the better you'll be able to handle the challenges the industry throws at you.

Is you're a super-thorough planner, you might like to brainstorm 'what if' scenarios, then rate them for their likelihood and impact. Focus on developing good plans for anything that's high likelihood and high impact.

You might like to consider what if:
- You get sick
- Your child/partner/family member gets sick
- A staff member gets sick
- A staff member suddenly can't get to work
- A customer gets injured in your cafe
- A customer has an anaphylactic reaction to your food
- You have a case of food poisoning
- The power goes off
- The coffee machine breaks down
- A supplier lets you down
- You experience an armed hold-up

Chapter 13: Lessons for the newbies

- You discover a staff member is stealing from you
- A client leaves without paying
- Your landlord won't renew the lease
- You get a bad review on social media
- You have a fire.

12. Beware of being so consumed by the work that you lose sight of the vision

In the everyday busyness of running a cafe, it's easy to lose sight of your longer-term vision.

In a cafe there's always work to be done. The physical work of selling and preparing food is relentless. Once the customers leave, you need to clean and close. Then there's all the business management to do – ordering, paying bills, paying staff, doing rosters, arranging maintenance, and so on.

If you allow it to, your cafe could take over every aspect of your life. And it's very easy to be so busy running the cafe that you forget to run the business.

Many cafe owners experience the same problem: they're so busy working in the business that they forget to work on the business. And the risk you face in this situation is that your cafe business won't end up being the business you'd originally planned to open.

My experience illustrates this problem. Anne-Maree and I planned to open a meetings venue with a small, simple cafe attached. But in employing chefs and deciding to cook everything on site, the cafe exploded and we found ourselves running a complex cafe attached to a struggling meetings venue. By the time we realised what we'd done, we were locked into arrangements that were difficult to undo.

You'll need to work in the business during its start-up phase, and you'll probably need to do every job that needs to be done. During start-up, expect to work very hard, with very long hours.

But as your business moves out of the start-up phase and begins to mature, you should be able to take a step back and reflect on the business itself. If you don't make the time to work on the business, you may find you never exit the start-up phase and never take full control of your vision.

13. Develop confidence in what you're doing

When you're a cafe newbie, it's easy to be concerned about whether your coffee and food are up to scratch. This is most likely to be a problem if you're a perfectionist and you expect yourself to get it right first time.

You need to develop confidence in your product and believe that you're offering value for money. Most importantly, you need to display confidence to your customers, even if you're quaking inside.

These thoughts may help to build your confidence:

- Your customers have no idea how you're feeling and they're probably not interested.
- Your customers are interested in the plate/cup put in front of them, not the terror you experienced creating it.
- Your customers are unlikely to watch you prepare their meal/drink, even in an open-plan cafe with an exposed kitchen.
- Few customers will congratulate you for a job well done (customers are more likely to complain than congratulate).
- If customers return, it's a sign they like what you're doing.

Don't listen to everyone's advice

You may find that you're astonished by how many customers are keen to tell you what you 'should' be doing. Don't fall into the trap of believing that other people know more about your business than you do. And don't fall into the trap of thinking you should test every idea that comes along.

Of course you need to listen to customer feedback and respond to customers' needs. That's the way to bring return business to your cafe.

But you also need enough confidence in what you're doing to be selective about the advice you listen to. This is your business and your vision. Implement ideas that are right for you and will help you achieve your vision. If you're feeling overwhelmed by the sheer volume of work involved in starting a cafe, resist the urge to feel that you must be failing because everyone suggests you try something new. Stick to the plan!

Enjoy your cafe journey!

Appendix 1
Business plan headings

These headings may help you to structure a business plan. Don't feel you need to include all these headings. If they're not relevant to your cafe, leave them out. And if you want to include something that doesn't fit under these headings, change the headings!

Remember, this is your business plan, designed to guide you in establishing your business. Include whatever detail you need to make your dream a reality.

The business
- Your business name, structure (e.g., company or family trust), vision, mission, and objectives

Premises
- This may include your search criteria for premises
- If you've found premises, this may include renovation plans, building approvals needed, or fitout details

Management and ownership
- You may want to summarise your background and experience (and that of any other owners) and whether you plan to work in the business

Personnel requirements
- Describe who will work in the cafe, what employees you need, how many hours a week of staffing you'll need, and how

you'll recruit and train staff (you may want to write position descriptions for staff and attach them to the plan)

Products and services
- Describe your product offerings

Market position
- Describe what you know about where your cafe will sit in the market, what gap you'll meet, and what demand you anticipate

Pricing strategy
- Include a broad statement about how price will position your cafe

Business issues
- You could discuss your cafe's growth potential and anything that may limit growth, any innovations you bring to the industry, your insurance requirements, your risk assessment, and any legal considerations

Business operations
- Describe how you'll work with suppliers and produce your products
- Identify any equipment needed
- Discuss your trading hours, payment types, credit policy, payments policy, quality control, warranties and refunds, affiliations, and memberships
- Discuss any issues relevant to your food business licensing (including the documentation required)

Sustainability plan
- Describe your efforts for environmental sustainability

The market
- Describe your market research, market targets, and any industry analysis (including a competitor analysis)

Customers
- Describe the customers you expect to attract

Appendix 1: Business plan headings

SWOT analysis
- Address the strengths and weaknesses of you and your cafe
- Address the opportunities and threats facing your cafe
- Include a discussion of how you'll address the weaknesses and threats and capitalise on the strengths and opportunities

Marketing, promotion, and advertising
- Summarise (or include) your promotion plan

Timeline
- Identify what tasks need to be done and when they'll happen – both in the lead-up to opening, and during the start-up phase

Finances
- Describe your financial objectives, financial assumptions, and financial goals

Appendix 2
Financial targets and ratios

Targets adopted for The Letter Lounge Cafe & Gifts

These are the targets I developed for The Letter Lounge Cafe & Gifts in early 2016. They suited the size of our cafe and the sales volume we hoped to achieve. We made most of our food on site (including our gluten-free bread, cakes, pies, and sausage rolls).

We didn't ever achieve these targets. Our wages costs were always far too high, because our cafe never achieved the sales targets we expected.

- Coffee sales for viability: 19 kg per week
- Coffee sales: 40% of turnover
- Purchase costs for food made off-site (including food cooked to order like bacon and eggs): 30% of sale price
- Ingredients costs for food made on site (e.g., baked goods): 12% of sale price (20% was more realistic)
- Wages: 20–25% of turnover
- Purchases: 35–38% of turnover

Industry averages reported by IBIS*World*[*]

As a percentage of turnover:
- Purchases: 35.5%
- Wages: 24.7%
- Rent: 10.8%

---

[*]Vuong, Bao. 2019, May. *Ibisworld Industry Report H4511b: Cafes and Coffee Shops in Australia*

Appendix 2: Financial targets and ratios

- Utilities: 2.2%
- Profit: 4.7%
- Coffee sales: 58.8%
- Food sales: 19.5%
- Other beverages: 21.7%

Appendix 3
Promotion plan headings and ideas

Your promotion plan should include:
- Goals (what you want to achieve)
- Audience (who you want to reach)
- Tools (what techniques you'll use)
- Timing
- Staffing (who will do the promotion work)
- Budget

Some ideas for promotional tools:
- Signage
- Website
- Social media presence
- Events
- Participation in local community events
- Electronic newsletter
- Printed materials (menu, flyer, business cards)
- Loyalty cards
- Special offers
- Local media stories
- Letterbox drops
- Window displays/signs
- Website listings
- Advertising

Appendix 3: Promotion plan headings and ideas

- Word-of-mouth – encourage customers to talk about you, particularly on social media

Appendix 4

Staff manual headings

Your staff manual could include these sections:
- Welcome to staff
- Contact details (of the shop and the managers)
- Trading hours
- Business purpose
- Our philosophy
- Charity partner
- Equal opportunity statement
- Award
- Your privacy
- Work hours
- Pay rate
- Performance review schedule
- Superannuation
- Termination and grievance procedures
- Appointment forms
- Union membership
- Staff meetings
- Training and skills development
- Dress and presentation
- Hygiene
- Sickness
- Smoking

Appendix 4: Staff manual headings

- Personal belongings storage
- Phone and internet access
- Social media
- Breaks
- Meals and drinks
- Injury
- Punctuality
- Toilet breaks
- Timesheets
- Pay schedule
- Customer interaction and service
- Phone etiquette
- Tips

Acknowledgements

A book about cafes is perhaps the most logical outcome for a writer–academic captivated by the cafe dream. Even though my dream cafe was short-lived, it provided me with a deep experience that more than compensates for the stress and financial pain. It left me with friendships and skills that I will value forever. Many, many people supported me through the cafe-to-book journey.

Thanks to the 10 cafe owners who generously shared their stories for this book. It's not always easy to tell a personal story, and I thank each cafe owner for their honesty and insight. Thanks also to cafe coach Simon O'Brien, who helped develop my thinking. Thanks to industry expert Christine Cottrell for her generous friendship and support. Thanks, too, to the many cafe owners who responded to my Facebook posts and online survey. Thanks to Sam McCulloch who responded to my Facebook call for someone to photograph Country Heart Cafe.

Our staff at The Letter Lounge Cafe & Gifts were a supportive, friendly bunch of people who believed in our dream and did what they could to make it a success. They generously shared their industry experience with their cafe-newbie employers. Our core team – Karen, Nathan, Eleanor, Val, Ali, Amber, Cassia, and Freyja – are vibrant, trustworthy, hardworking, and genuinely likeable people. Our other staff who, for various reasons, didn't stay with us for long, also helped to establish our business and develop our industry knowledge – Jacinta,

Lainie, Shari, and Thalia. Our two marketing interns – Ken and Brigit – worked hard to put our fledgling business in the public eye.

At The Letter Lounge we worked with some very special suppliers, contractors, and customers who helped us to find our feet in the industry, supported us when things got tough, and helped us to host some incredible events. Special thanks to Michael McLaren for guidance that went well beyond the renovation and start-up phase and to Peter Clifford for rescuing us on more than one occasion. Thanks to all the staff at Elixir Coffee for patiently helping us to learn how to work with coffee. Thanks to the special customers who visited regularly and gave us moments when we really did live the cafe dream. Thanks to all the people who held their events at our lovely venue.

Kirsty and Patrice from Brisbane Self Publishing Service helped to create this book's finished form and connected me with an extended network through the Brisbane Authors Networking Group. The writers who attend the Shut Up & Write group I host each month gave me the motivation needed to finish.

Special thanks to my family for being with me on this journey. Thanks, Anne-Maree, for agreeing that a cafe sounded like a good idea, for coming along for the ride, and for supporting me to write this book. Thanks Carwyn and Emrys, for coping with our chaotic business, the major change to your lifestyles, and suddenly absent parents. Thanks to my extended family for their encouragement.

About Judy Gregory

Dr Judy Gregory is a writer, editor, researcher, and former cafe dreamer. She and her partner operated The Letter Lounge Cafe & Gifts in Brisbane's Red Hill from March 2016 until May 2018. *Newbies in the cafe* is the book she wishes she had read before embarking on her cafe dream.

Judy lives in Brisbane with her partner Anne-Maree, their two teenage sons, and their 10-year-old dog Laika (named for the first dog sent into space).

Closing The Letter Lounge sadly brought to an end Judy's daily interaction with a La Marzocco Linea PB espresso machine. In its place, today she uses a cafetière, with 22 g of freshly ground coffee to 8 oz of not-quite-boiling water, brewed for exactly 5 minutes.

www.ingramcontent.com/pod-product-compliance
Lightning Source LLC
Chambersburg PA
CBHW040241010526
44107CB00065B/2825